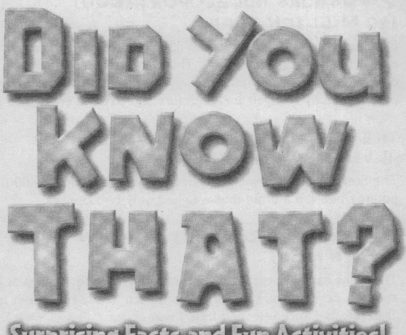

DID YOU KNOW THAT?

Surprising Facts and Fun Activities!

Published by Playmor... ...t, 2nd
Floor, Hackensack, ...hing
Corp., 570 Seve... ...8

Copyright © MMV Playmore inc., ...d
Waldman Publishing Corp., New York, New York

The Playmore/Waldman® and Bug Logo® are registered
trademarks of Playmore Inc., Publishers and
Waldman Publishing Corp.,New York, New York

Printed in Canada

DINOSAURS RULED FOR ABOUT 140 MILLION YEARS.

Dinosaurs lived between 250 and 65 million years ago. For most of that time, they dominated Earth. Then, almost overnight, they disappeared. Some scientists believe that the Earth's climate may have drastically changed and dinosaurs couldn't find enough to eat.

THE STEGOSAURUS DINOSAUR HAD A VERY SMALL BRAIN.

The Stegosaurus was a big dinosaur. It weighed almost 4,000 pounds, but had a brain that weighed only two ounces.

THE TRICERATOPS HAD A HORN ON ITS NOSE.

The plant-eating Triceratops had three horns, one over each eye and one on its nose. The horns were each nearly three feet long. Triceratops ("three-horned face") was about 20 feet tall and 30 feet long.

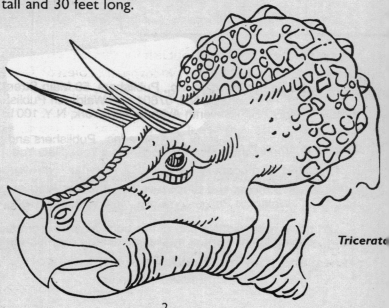

Triceratо

SOME DINOSAURS HAD SELF-SHARPENING TEETH.

Certain dinosaurs ate only plants. They had self-sharpening teeth. As the dinosaur chewed its vegetables, its upper and lower teeth ground against each other. In this way the dinosaur's teeth were kept sharp.

DINOSAURS TRAVELED IN HERDS.

Like elephants, many dinosaurs lived in herds. They kept their young at the center of the herd to protect them, just as elephant herds do today.

FAST FACT The 20-foot-long, 1,700-pound Utahraptor had claws that were 12 inches long.

Rescue the Dinosaur Hunter

Just before he was able to publish his discoveries of some new fossils, rival dinosaur hunters kidnapped Professor Tennessee Smith, the famous dinosaur hunter. Fortunately, he was able to smuggle out a note that revealed what he found. But it's in code. Look at the note and see if you can figure out the clues. If you break the code, you'll be able to learn:

1. What kind of dinosaurs he found. 2. In what form some of the fossils were. 3. What the dinosaurs ate. 4. What kind of groups the dinosaurs traveled in. 5. What the dinosaurs had on their heads.

"Help! My captors have big egos. They are flying in planes, and they are making me eat hard corns!"

3   Solution, see page 134

ONE OF THE LARGEST DINOSAURS ATE 900 POUNDS OF FOOD A DAY.

Brachiosaurus, a plant-eater, was about 40 feet tall and 70 feet long. It may have weighed as much as 80 tons. All it ate was vegetation—almost a half ton of plants every day.

THE LARGEST DINOSAUR EGGS EVER FOUND WERE ALMOST A FOOT LONG.

All dinosaurs laid eggs, but some laid truly huge eggs. The eggs of the 100-million-year-old Hypselosaurus were 12 inches long and 10 inches wide. One of its eggs could weigh 16 pounds.

SOME VERY FAST DINOSAURS COULD OUTRUN A RUNNING OSTRICH.

The meat-eating dinosaur Ornithomimus ran about 30 miles per hour, or as fast as an ostrich. Gallimimus, a dinosaur that ran on long hind legs, probably reached a speed of 35 miles per hour, as fast as a horse at full gallop.

DINOSAURS HAD LOTS OF BIG TEETH.

The meat-eating dinosaur Tyrannosaurus rex had teeth that were six inches long, which went along nicely with its 14,000 pounds and 18-foot height. Tyrannosaurus rex was about 40 feet long. Hadrosaurs had more than 2,000 teeth. When old ones wore out, new ones quickly grew in. Hadrasaurs may have looked like today's ducks. Their name, from Latin, means "duck-billed." A Hadrosaur was about 20 feet long and six feet tall.

FAST FACT The biggest dinosaurs were vegetarians. These included the Apatosaurus, which weighed more than 30 tons.

MOST DINOSAUR FOSSILS IN THE UNITED STATES HAVE BEEN FOUND IN FOUR STATES.

Dinosaur fossils have been found in many states. Colorado, Wyoming, Utah, and Montana lead in the number of dinosaur fossils found.

Dino Egg Hunt

There are eight dinosaur eggs hidden in this picture. Can you find them all? As you find the eggs, circle them.

Solution, see page 134

Bees work very hard for their honey.

To make one pound of honey, worker bees must visit and tap about two million flowers.

Some spiders change color.

Not all spiders spin webs to catch their prey. Crab spiders ambush theirs. They wait on flowers until an insect lands and then they seize it. Crab spiders disguise themselves by changing their color to match the color of the flower on which they are waiting.

Goliath bird-eating spiders have 11-inch leg spans.

The truly big goliath bird-eating tarantula spiders of South America weigh more than three ounces and have a leg span of more than 11 inches. They are the largest spiders known. They outweigh many birds, which weigh only two or three ounces.

Dragonflies were once the largest creatures in the air.

Millions of years ago, giant dragonflies ruled the air. They had wingspans of about 29 inches.

Dragonfly

6

Cockroaches are very old and very fast.

Species of cockroaches existed 300 million years ago and remain practically unchanged today. A cockroach can run about 32 inches per second, which is the same as 2 miles per hour. This is the same as a lion running at about 70 miles per hour.

Male fireflies attract females through a form of Morse code.

The male firefly sends out a specific flash pattern of light as a signal. Some species can generate both red and green light. Fireflies, which are actually beetles, not flies, produce a chemical called luciferin that reacts with oxygen to create light.

The female common housefly lays from 600 to 1,000 eggs in her lifetime.

Most fly species lay eggs five to 25 times a year.

FAST FACT An ant can carry a pebble 50 times its own weight.

What's Bugging You?

Unscramble the letters to find words about bugs.

1. ebe _____
2. repids _____
3. lyf _____
4. tna _____
5. rocccohak _____

Solution, see page 134

Crabs use camouflage to hide from enemies.

Crabs are masters of disguise. They're sand-colored so they are hard to see on the seabed. Decorator crabs, or spider crabs, actually collect, cut, skillfully arrange, and cement algae, seaweed, and sea creatures on to their shells so that they look like part of the ocean floor.

Some crabs use shells as trailer homes.

Hermit crabs have no shell on their long, soft abdomens, so they have to find empty snail shells for protection. They drag these shells behind them like house trailers as they move about. If threatened, they retreat into the shell. Their enlarged right claw acts as a door, blocking off the opening of the shell from enemies.

FAST FACT The horseshoe crab is not a crab. Its closest relative is the spider.

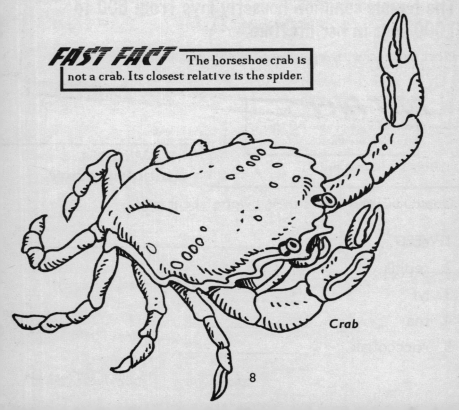

Crab

8

Crab fisheries are centuries old.

Crab fisheries are among the oldest industries in the United States. Crabbing for the blue crab was done in Chesapeake Bay as far back as the 1630s.

Crabs and water fleas are cousins, and they've got a big family.

Crabs, lobsters, crayfish, shrimps, barnacles, and water fleas are all crustaceans. There are more than 30,000 species of crustaceans.

Crab Quiz

Fill in each blank with the correct "crab" word.

1. SMALL SOUR FRUIT _____

2. GROUCHY _____

3. WEED _____

4. SIDEWAYS _____

Solution, see page 134

There is a frog that sweats deadly poison.

The skin secretions of the golden poison dart frog of South America is the strongest biotoxin. A biotoxin is a poisonous substance made by an animal or plant. An adult golden poison dart frog contains enough poison to kill about 2,200 people.

The giant anaconda is the heaviest snake in the world.

The heaviest snake is the anaconda of tropical South America. It can weigh up to 500 pounds and stretch out to 30 feet. The anaconda, which is not poisonous, attacks deer and caimans. Caimans are members of the crocodile family. Anacondas also crawl into trees to feed on birds.

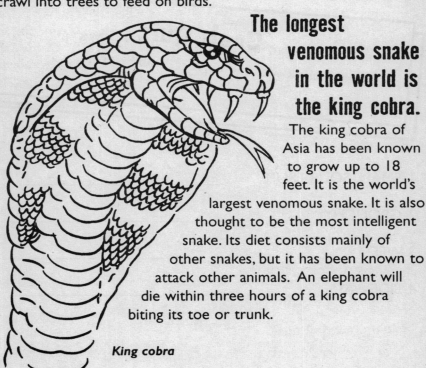

The longest venomous snake in the world is the king cobra.

The king cobra of Asia has been known to grow up to 18 feet. It is the world's largest venomous snake. It is also thought to be the most intelligent snake. Its diet consists mainly of other snakes, but it has been known to attack other animals. An elephant will die within three hours of a king cobra biting its toe or trunk.

King cobra

Rattlesnakes are born with temporary rattles.

Rattlesnakes are born with a temporary small rattle at the end of their bodies. This temporary rattle is called a prerattle and it is shed a few days after the snake has been born. In its place grows the first part of the rattle called the button. As the snake grows, the rattle will grow more rings or segments.

FAST FACT The rattlesnake's rattle can be heard up to 30 miles away.

"Badder" Adders

These are pairs of rhyming words. Can you figure out the right pairs to fit the clues?
Here is an example: Which two rhyming words could mean "cook a crawler"? Answer: Bake snake.

Which two rhyming words could mean:

1. A fishing python?

2. A shoplifting asp?

3. A serpent's sirloin?

4. A fang's cubicle?

5. A fighting snake?

Solution, see page 134

The largest freshwater fish is a catfish.

A giant catfish from Southeast Asia is the world's largest freshwater fish. It averages 350 pounds and eight feet in length.

The largest saltwater fish lives on tiny plants.

The whale shark, which eats only microscopic plankton, is the world's largest saltwater fish. A whale shark may measure more than 50 feet in length and weigh more than 20 tons. It is mild-mannered and has even been ridden by divers.

The "man-eater" shark is the world's largest carnivorous fish.

The extremely dangerous great white shark is the largest carnivorous fish in the world. This super predator can reach more than 26 feet in length and weigh as much as 5,000 pounds.

The anglerfish uses an electric bulb as bait.

The deep-sea anglerfish has long filaments with a light on the end, which dangles over the top of its head. Other fish mistake the light for food and swim into the anglerfish's huge mouth. The anglerfish is able to produce chemicals that allow it to give off light or a glow. This is called bioluminescence. With its enormous mouth and expandable stomach, an anglerfish can swallow other fish as large as itself.

FAST FACT A blue whale can eat about 40 million krill a day—about 8,000 pounds of food.

The giant squid can reach a length of 60 feet including tentacles.

Giant squid have eyes the size of basketballs. They are the favorite food of giant sperm whales, themselves the largest carnivorous animals in the world. When being chased, many squid squirt a dark liquid to distract their attackers so they can escape.

The largest animals of all time eat tiny shrimp.

The blue whale, the biggest animal ever to live on Earth, weighs about 300,000 pounds and can grow to almost 100 feet in length. Its main diet are small shrimp-like creatures called krill, which are each smaller than one inch.

Find the Real Catfish

Only one of these three fish is a real catfish. Can you find the real one?

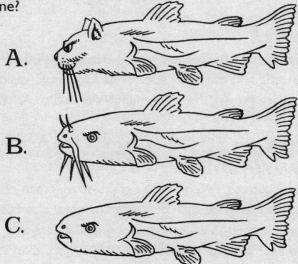

A.

B.

C.

Solution, see page 134

The largest bird can't fly

The ostrich, at more than eight feet tall and 350 pounds, is the tallest and heaviest bird, but it does not fly. It can run at about 35 miles per hour. The wild turkey runs 30 miles per hour, the California roadrunner runs 26 miles per hour, and the common pheasant has been clocked at 21 miles per hour.

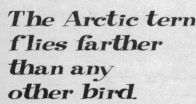

Ostrich

The Arctic tern flies farther than any other bird

Every year, the Arctic tern makes a round-trip of 25,000 miles between the Arctic and the Antarctic. It nests in Arctic regions, and when its young are grown, the whole family flies off to Antarctica.

Albatrosses live longer than most other birds in the wild

The wandering albatross, which has the greatest wingspan of any bird, is believed to live more than 80 years. The royal albatross has a lifespan of more than 60 years. In captivity, the sulfur-crested cockatoo, a popular pet, has been known to live more than 75 years.

The smartest birds are members of the crow family.

Of about the 10,000 species of birds in the world, the most intelligent are crows and their cousins: ravens, jackdaws, jays, and magpies. They can be taught, very quickly, to speak.

Hummingbirds drink nectar at the rate of about 13 licks per second.

As the tiny hummingbird hovers like a helicopter in front of a flower, it uses its long, extendible tongue to reach nectar deep within the flower.

FAST FACT The Portuguese word for hummingbird is *beija-flor,* which means "kiss-flower."

There's a Bird in My Word

Some words contain other words inside them. For instance, the word "lady" contains the words "lady" and "lad." Find the bird words hidden in these words:

1. Find a bird inside the word **eternally**.
2. Find a bird inside the word **hyphenation**.
3. Find a bird inside the word **bowling**.
4. Find a bird inside the word **crowded**.
5. Find a bird inside the word **gullible**.
6. Find a bird inside the word **stealing**.
7. Find a bird inside the word **beagle**.
8. Find a bird inside the word **regretted**.
9. Find a bird inside the word **craven**.
10. Find a bird inside the word **probing**.

Solution, see page 134

SOME TINY SHREWS HAVE POISONOUS SALIVA.

The small, mouse-like shrew has sharp teeth and some of these bloodthirsty animals have poisonous saliva for stunning prey. A shrew's heart may beat 1,200 times per minute, and a highly nervous shrew may die from the shock of a loud noise.

TIGERS EAT A LOT.

A tiger can eat about 40 pounds of meat in one sitting. Then, they usually do not eat again for several days. Tigers in zoos only eat about 10 pounds of meat per day.

VAMPIRE BATS SOMETIMES SUCK BLOOD FROM HUMANS.

While South American vampire bats usually suck blood from livestock, they will occasionally go after humans. To survive, vampire bats must drink a teaspoonful of blood per night. Their saliva contains a powerful blood thinner that is 20 times stronger than any other blood thinner known. This thinner keeps the blood from clotting and makes it easier for the bat to drink it. This substance is used to make a drug for heart attack patients. The medicine is called Draculin.

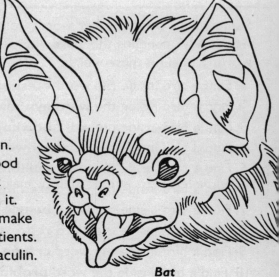

Bat

THE WALRUS CAN DIVE AS FAR AS 350 FEET BELOW THE SURFACE OF THE ARCTIC WATERS.

For all their size, two-ton walruses are very fast swimmers, reaching a top speed of 25 miles per hour. They use their heads to break breathing holes in ice up to eight inches thick. Then they use their long tusks to widen the holes.

FAST FACT Tigers can jump up to 33 feet in one leap.

For Openers

Just add one or more letters to a word to make another word, without changing the order of the letters.

Here is an example: Add a letter to a seed to make a liquid quantity. Answer: pit = pint.

1. Add a letter to your hearing organ to make a grizzly.

2. Add two letters to what is yours to make a kind of weasel.

3. Add two letters to plus to make an African antelope.

4. Add a letter to writing fluid to make a kind of weasel.

5. Add a letter to arrived to make a dromedary.

6. Add a letter to an artist's stand to make a ferret.

Solution, see page 134

Dogs were domesticated before cats.

Wolves—the ancestors of all dog breeds today—lived with humans as far back as 12,000 years ago. Cats took their time about it and decided to move in with humans about 8,000 years ago.

The first dog license cost $2.00.

New York was the first state to license dogs. On March 8, 1894, the American Society for the Prevention of Cruelty to Animals (ASPCA) was authorized by New York State to collect a $2.00 license fee for dogs in cities with human populations over one million.

Dogs Can See in Color.

Dogs are not totally color-blind. They just cannot see the colors red or orange, and they don't see colors as distinctly as humans can. Smell, not sight, is a dog's sharpest sense.

Dogs nap rather than sleep.

Dogs, like all animals, are light sleepers. So while dogs seem to spend a lot of time snoozing, they're really napping rather than slumbering. That's why they can wake up so quickly when you call to them.

German shepherd

Dogs have more chromosomes than humans.

Each body cell in a dog contains 39 pairs of the heredity-carrying structures called chromosomes. This is more than any other animal, including man, who has only 23 pairs. A dog also has more teeth (42) than man (32).

FAST FACT The chow-chow is the only dog with a blue tongue.

What Kind of Dog Is That?

Can you identify these dogs from the clues provided?

Here is an example: This 18-letter dog starts with an R and ends with a K, and it fights lions in Africa.
Answer: Rhodesian Ridgeback.

1. This six-letter dog starts with a C and ends with an E, and it herds sheep.

2. This five-letter dog starts with a B and ends with an R, and it comes out swinging.

3. This nine-letter dog starts with a C and ends with an A, and it comes from a state in Mexico.

4. This nine-letter dog starts with a G and ends with a D, and it takes a bus to work.

Solution, see page 135

The smallest cats come from Singapore.

The smallest breed of domestic cat is the Singapura or "drain cat" of Singapore. Adult males average six pounds in weight and adult females four pounds.

Ancient Egyptians did not worship cats, they adored them!

The ancient Egyptians were very fond of cats. Cats were cherished members of the household. When a fire broke out in an Egyptian household, people would be more concerned about saving the cats than putting out the fire. Despite the immense popularity of cats, the ancient Egyptians did not worship the animal itself. Instead, they paid homage to Bast, a cat-headed goddess. However, they did mummify their cats—by the thousands!

Bast, the Egyptian cat goddess

The cat is the only animal that purrs.

A cat can cry, hiss, and growl, and so can a lot of other animals. But the cat is unique: It's the only animal capable of purring. How it accomplishes this is still a mystery.

Cats don't have nine lives.

Because cats are so agile and athletic and can get out of danger so quickly, people say that cats have lives to spare.

Catty Words

How many words can you think of for the word "cat?"

1. How many seven-letter words can you think of for breeds of cat? (We know three.)

2. How many four-letter words can you think of for breeds of cat? (We know one.)

3. How many 13-letter words can you think of for breeds of cat? (We know three.)

FAST FACT The cat has fewer side teeth than any other mammal.

Solution, see page 135

The heaviest of all woods is black ironwood.

Black ironwood, also called South African ironwood, weighs up to 93 pounds per cubic foot.

The largest seed is the double coconut.

The double coconut from the Seychelles islands in the Indian Ocean weighs 40 pounds, making it the largest seed in the world.

The monkey bread tree is big but not tall.

The monkey bread tree, or baobab, grows broad without growing tall. Its trunk may be 30 feet in diameter but only 60 feet high, the height of a large maple tree. It has branches as thick as the trunks of most trees.

Bo tree

The world's tallest flowering plant is from Australia.

The mountain ash of Australia, a southern eucalyptus, grows higher than any other flowering plant. Its height can exceed 325 feet.

The bo tree of Sri Lanka is revered by Buddhists.

A sacred bo tree, or pipal, in Sri Lanka is paid homage to by Buddhists. It is said that it was planted 2,200 years ago from a branch of the original sacred bo tree under which Buddha gained enlightenment.

The raffia palm has the largest leaves of any plant.

The leaves of Madagascar's raffia palm grow up to 65 feet in length. The raffia palm can also be found in parts of Africa.

FAST FACT Wood from the tropical lignum vitae tree is so heavy it can't float in water. It's used to make judges' mallets.

Look at the Tree

A tree has many parts. See how many you can find from the list in this box. Look down and across.

Leaf Branch Stem Trunk Root Twig

```
T W I G Q V W H E R
X T R U N K D O X O
S L E A F H F D R O
T W E Q R I Z E V T
E B R A N C H B E I
M A L Q P F G T U J
```

The oldest living tree is in California.

The oldest tree is believed to be a bristle cone pine tree in the White Mountains of California. It is estimated to be almost 5,000 years old.

The largest known tree is in California.

The General Sherman giant sequoia growing in Sequoia National Park, California, is the biggest living tree in the world. It is 275 feet tall. Its diameter is 36 feet. Its branches are up to seven feet thick. Its weight is estimated to be over four million pounds. It is almost 4,000 years old.

The silver maple is the most common tree in the United States.

The silver maple, which often grows to 130 feet in height in damp areas, is the most common tree in the United States.

There's more peat moss in Russia than anywhere else.

Peat moss is used as packing material for shipping plants. It grows in swamps or bogs. Russia's Vasyugan Swamp, on the world's largest plain (the West Siberian Plain), has more peat moss than any other swamp. Peat moss is also known as sphagnum.

Some bamboos grow up to three feet a day.

Bamboo grows quickly. One Indian variety may grow to be more than 100 feet tall. Some bamboos flower only every 100 years.

FAST FACT Russia has more forests than any other country. with 23 million square miles of trees.

'mazing Tree

Can you get to the top of the General Sherman sequoia and find your way down again?

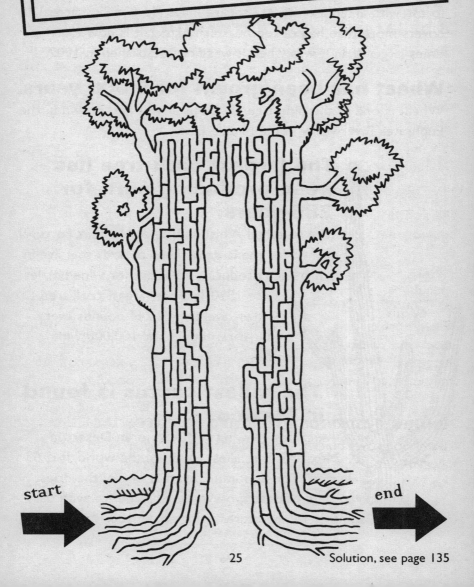

start

end

Solution, see page 135

The largest national forest in the United States is larger than the entire state of West Virginia.

Tongass National Forest in Sitka, Alaska, is our largest national forest, with an area of 25,937 square miles (16.6 million acres). It covers more than half of southeastern Alaska. It is now four times larger than it was when it was first established in 1902.

Wheat has been grown for 9,000 years.

Wheat is one of the oldest cereal crops. It was first grown in the Euphrates River Valley in the Middle East.

The largest cork tree has been producing cork for 285 years.

The so-called Whistler Tree of Alentejo, Portugal, named for the large number of birds that live in it, has been producing raw cork for wine bottles since 1820. It is the largest cork tree known, averaging 2,244 pounds every nine years, enough for 100,000 wine bottles.

Cactus

The tallest cactus is found in Mexico.

A cactus growing in the Sonoran Desert in Mexico is the tallest cactus in the world. It is 63 feet tall. The Sonoran Desert is one of the driest and hottest spots in North America, with daily summer temperatures rising above 100° Fahrenheit.

Woody Riddle

To solve the Woody Riddle, fill in the answers to the clues, with one letter in each space. Then transfer those letters to the boxes with matching numbers below. When all the boxes are filled in, you will find the answer to the Woody Riddle. (Hint: It's a job that has something to do with trees!)

A. __ __ __   Haze or confusion.
   1 2 10

B. __ __ __ __   Hard to find, or a way to cook meat.
   3 8 7 11

C. __ __ __ __ __   Back of a ship, or very strict.
   5 6 4 12 9

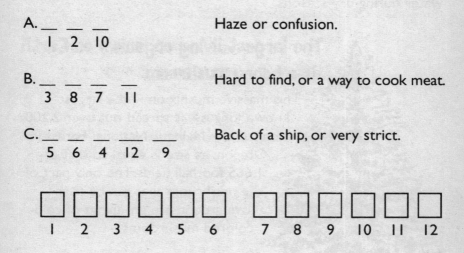

☐ ☐ ☐ ☐ ☐ ☐   ☐ ☐ ☐ ☐ ☐ ☐
1 2 3 4 5 6   7 8 9 10 11 12

FAST FACT The pharaohs of ancient Egypt were buried with a supply of wheat to keep them fed during their voyage into the afterlife.

Solution, see page 135

There are more than 500,000 different kinds of plants.

So far, botanists (plant scientists) have discovered more than 500,000 different species of plants. Each year, about 2,000 new plants are discovered.

A watermelon is mostly water.

More than 90 percent of a watermelon is water. In very dry parts of Africa, it's especially grown to serve as an emergency source of water during dry seasons.

The largest living organism on Earth is a honey mushroom.

This massive mushroom—the largest known fungus—is spread out over 2,200 acres in the Malheur National Forest in Oregon. Its size is equal to that of 1,665 football fields. The only part of the mushroom that can be seen above ground are groupings of gold-colored mushrooms.

The potato was first grown in the United States less than 300 years ago.

The earliest authentic record of the potato's cultivation, in the United States, is dated 1719, at Londonderry, New Hampshire.

Evergreen tree

Needles keep evergreen trees green all year round.

Evergreens have leaves shaped like needles. These needles are waxed and don't lose a lot of moisture and fall off in winter the way leaves from other trees do. The needle leaves of evergreens stay put longer, so the evergreen tree stays green longer.

A caterpillar makes the Mexican jumping bean jump.

A little caterpillar living inside the Mexican jumping bean feeds on the bean, jumping and rolling as it eats, thus causing the bean to move.

FAST FACT Botanists believe there are another 500,000 plant species around the world still waiting to be discovered.

Double-Meaning Plants

The names of certain plants, trees, shrubs, and flowers have more than one meaning. From the clues given below, figure out the words.

Here is an example: Which word means both a tree and a cinder? Answer: Ash

1. Which word means both a part of the eye and a flower?

2. Which word means both a wise man and an herb?

3. Which word means both neat and a tree?

4. Which word means both daddy and a flower?

5. Which word means both jump and a flower?

Solution, see page 135

Luther Burbank invented 220 plants.

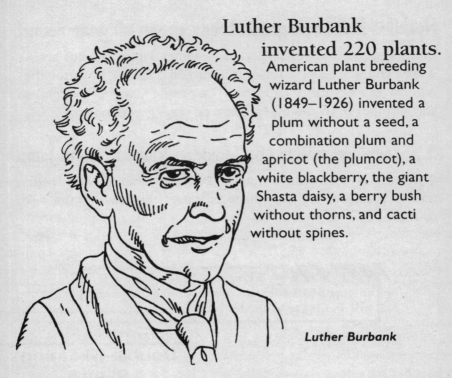

American plant breeding wizard Luther Burbank (1849–1926) invented a plum without a seed, a combination plum and apricot (the plumcot), a white blackberry, the giant Shasta daisy, a berry bush without thorns, and cacti without spines.

Luther Burbank

Rubber, sugar, maple syrup, frankincense, and myrrh have a lot in common.

Rubber, sugar, maple syrup, frankincense, and myrrh all have "sappy" beginnings. Maple syrup comes from the sap of maple trees. Rubber is made from latex, the sap of the rubber tree. Sugar comes from the sap of sugarcane, a type of grass. And the spices frankincense and myrrh come from the sap of desert plants in the Middle East.

FAST FACT Luther Burbank was friends with two other great American inventors. Thomas Edison and Henry Ford.

Teak furniture lasts for 1,000 years.

Furniture made from the wood of the teak tree can last for more than 1,000 years. The teak tree grows in Asia. In some places, elephants are used to carry and pile the heavy teak logs.

The resurrection plant rolls around, looking for water.

Resurrection plants are certain types of plants including the rose of Jericho. The resurrection plant doesn't die like other plants when it runs out of water. Instead, it rolls itself up into a tight little ball and gets blown around by the wind until it finds a nice wet spot. There it unfolds and releases its seeds. Resurrection plants are found growing in very dry places, such as Texas, Mexico, and Africa.

Garden Fun

There are four flowers and fruits planted in the sentences below. Each one reads across two words. Can you dig them all?

1. When she won the Oscar, nationwide ticket sales to her movies soared.

2. "Before you order the ban, analyze the people's reaction," suggested the king's adviser.

3. "James Bond paid for my garden," Ian Fleming said.

4. "Check my schedule, Monday," the busy executive ordered.

 Solution, see page 136

The daisy was a sign of the sun to the ancient British.

Because of its long white rays and yellow center, the ancient British thought the daisy was like a tiny sun. That's why they called it the "day's eye." Their term became our word "daisy."

A prairie plant helps lost people find their way.

The leaves of the compass plant, found in the prairie states, always point north or south. Pioneers who got lost were able to get their bearings from this handy plant.

Compass plant

There's a tree that looks like a butcher's display.

The 20-foot-high sausage tree of West Africa bears fruit that look like dangling giant sausages. Although these "sausages" can't be eaten, they are used in traditional folk medicine.

FAST FACT An example of the compass plant is prickly lettuce, an ancestor of garden lettuce.

The upas tree was once thought to breathe out poison.

The 150-foot-high upas tree of tropical Asia was once believed to have a poisonous breath that killed any creature in its vicinity. While that's not true, it is a fact that the upas tree has a deadly sap that is used for arrow poison.

A kind of cucumber squirts its seeds 20 feet.

The squirting cucumber squirts out its seeds 20 feet or more. The plant is a relative of the garden cucumber.

The Rhyming Plant Puzzle

All the words below rhyme with the word "plant." Place them in the diagram so they connect just like in a crossword. When you have completed the puzzle, you will have used each word once. To start you off, we've filled in one word.

ANT	CHANT	GRANT	RANT
AUNT	ENCHANT	PANT	SCANT
CANT	GALLANT	~~PLANT~~	SLANT

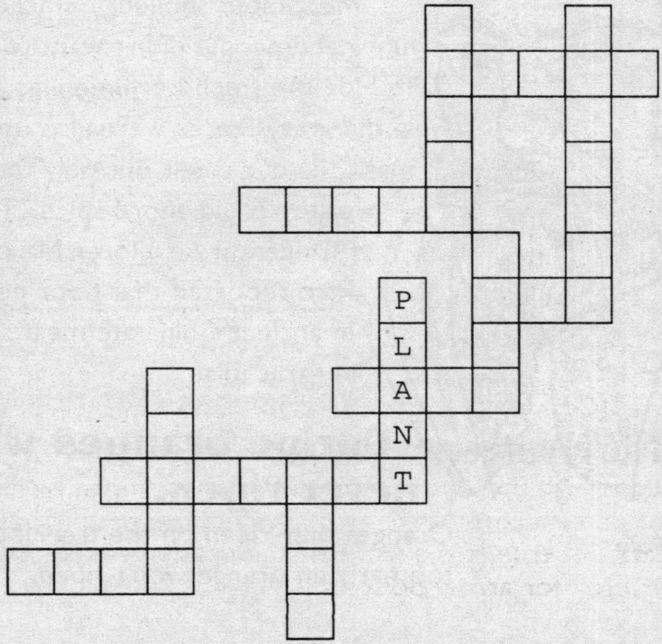

Solution, see page 136

Peanuts grow underground.

Instead of growing above the ground, peanuts develop under the soil. They grow there for four or five months before they're ready to be harvested.

The onion was a sign of the universe to the ancient Egyptians.

Because of its round bulb, the ancient Egyptians thought that the onion was the perfect symbol of the universe. The word "onion" comes from the Latin *unus*, meaning "one."

Meat was once doused with perfume before being served.

Before the days of refrigeration, meat often spoiled. It smelled funny and people didn't want to eat it. To hide the smell, perfume was added to the gravy. Spices were also used to mask the bad smell. But only the wealthy could afford spices. The 13th-century explorer Marco Polo reported that poor people in ancient China ate meat soaked in garlic juice.

Marco Polo

Unripe oranges will never ripen.

Oranges only ripen on the tree. If picked too early, an orange won't ripen.

Tea bags were invented to cheaply ship tea.

At one time, tea was shipped in large, heavy tin cans. A New York tea merchant wanted to send samples of his tea to customers, so he decided to sew the tea inside small cloth bags and send them that way. The customers wanted more of the new tea bags. Now tea bags are made of a special paper.

The first cookbook came from Rome.

The first known cookbook was written in Rome, Italy, by Marcus Gavius Apicius in the first century AD.

> **FAST FACT** The earliest cookbook in English is *The Forme of Cury* (Forms of Cookery), written in about 1390.

Scramble Puzzle

In each clue below, the word "scramble" has been substituted for another word that has to do with preparing food. The word remains the same for each clue. Each clue tells you a little more about "scramble." See if you can figure out what "scramble" is, before clue # 4.

1. "Scrambled" eggs should really be simmered.

2. "A stew 'scrambled' is a stew spoiled."

3. Every cook should know how to "scramble" water.

4. A watched pot never "scrambles."

Solution, see page 136

Broad beans are the oldest vegetable known.

The broad bean, also known as vetch, has been grown since prehistoric times. It was the only bean known in Europe before 1492.

A French candy maker invented canning.

French candy maker and distiller Nicolas-François Appert was the man who found a way, in 1810, of preserving cooked food in containers. The French government awarded him 12,000 francs for his invention.

Water makes popcorn pop.

Popcorn kernels have water in them. When the kernels are heated, this water turns to steam. The steam pushes its way against the walls of the kernel which explodes, making the popping sound.

Some recipes are older than you think.

The earliest recipes, which date from 1700 BC, were found in Iraq. One recipe was for a bird cooked with onion, garlic, and milk.

The Egyptians were the first bakers.

By 2600 BC, the ancient Egyptians had perfected the art of baking bread.

The most nutritious fruit is the avocado.

The avocado contains more than 740 calories per edible pound and as much as 22 percent oil, the second-highest percentage of oil in any fruit after the olive. It contains thiamine, riboflavin, vitamin A, and up to two percent protein.

Chocolate was once the drink of emperors.

In 1519, the Aztec emperor Montezuma (c. 1466–1520) proudly served a drink called chocolatl to Hernando Cortés (1485–1547), the Spanish conqueror of Mexico.

Montezuma

FAST FACT The ancient Greeks called the ancient Egyptians the "bread eaters."

Food Fillings

Fill in the missing letter to complete each food item.

1. cho__olate

2. __vocado

3. bre__d

4. pop__orn

5. b__an

Solution, see page 136

THE FARTHEST VISIBLE OBJECT IN THE SKY WAS CHARTED 3,000 YEARS AGO.

The most remote heavenly body visible to the naked eye is a spiral galaxy in the constellation Andromeda known as M31. Astronomers charted it as far back as 905 BC. It is about 12.6 quintillion miles from Earth. It contains more than 300 billion stars, and its mass is estimated at more than 350 billion times greater than that of our sun. Its brightness is equal to 11 billion suns.

SATURN HAS THE MOST SATELLITES, OR MOONS, OF ANY PLANET.

Of the nine planets in our solar system, all but Venus and Mercury have natural satellites. The planet with the most is Saturn, with at least 18 moons. Earth and Pluto are the only planets with a single satellite. The solar system has a total of 63 known satellites.

Saturn and its moons

THE STAR BETELGEUSE FLUCTUATES IN SIZE.

Betelgeuse (the reddish star that marks the right shoulder of the constellation Orion) is 300 light-years away. Betelgeuse is one of the largest stars in the sky. Betelgeuse's size changes, from a minimum diameter of 500 times that of the sun to a maximum diameter of about 920 times that of the sun.

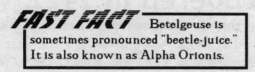

FAST FACT Betelgeuse is sometimes pronounced "beetle-juice." It is also known as Alpha Orionis.

Watch the Sky

Unscramble the letters to find words about heavenly bodies.

1. rats _____

2. xygala _____

3. netpla _____

4. liletaset _____

 Solution, see page 137

The smallest star is smaller than Earth.

The white dwarf star L362-81 has an estimated diameter of 3,500 miles, or less than half of that of Earth. A white dwarf is a star that has collapsed into a super-dense ball of matter.

The star nearest to Earth was discovered in 1915.

The nearest star is the very faint red dwarf star Proxima Centauri, discovered in 1915. A red dwarf is a star that is small and cool in temperature. It is 4.22 light-years (24,800,000,000,000 miles) away. Its weight is only one-tenth that of the sun. The nearest "star" visible to the naked eye is Alpha Centauri. It is actually a triple star system. It is 4.35 light-years away.

The Olympus Mons volcano on Mars

The brightest star is a dog.

Sirius A (Alpha Canis Majoris), also known as the Dog Star, is the brightest star of the 6,000 visible in the heavens. It is 40 times more luminous than the sun.

The most spectacular surface feature on any planet is on Mars.

The highest and most spectacular surface feature on Mars is a gigantic volcano, Olympus Mons. It has a diameter of 345 miles and soars 85,000 feet above the surrounding plain.

FAST FACT Uranus has 15 moons. The ice cliff on the moon Miranda is 65.000 feet high.

Which One Does Not Belong?

One item in each of these groups is an intruder. Do you know which one it is?

1. planet, star, moon, spaceship _____

2. Mars, Mercury, Jupiter, Odin _____

3. light-year, white dwarf, red dwarf, purple grape _____

The brightest planet in the solar system is Venus.

Viewed from Earth, Venus is by far the brightest of the five planets visible to the naked eye. The faintest is Pluto. Uranus is only barely visible.

The largest moon in our Solar System is more than 2,000 times the size of Earth's moon.

The largest and heaviest moon, or satellite, is Ganymede (Jupiter III), which is 2.017 times heavier than our moon and has a diameter of 3,270 miles. The smallest satellite is Leda (Jupiter XIII) with a diameter of 9.3 miles.

There are two crabs in the sky, one bright and the other dim.

Cancer (Latin for "crab") is a zodiacal constellation that is not easy to locate because it has no bright stars. It was known as the Crab in the Sky to many ancient peoples.

The other heavenly crab is the Crab Nebula, a crab-shaped supernova remnant, or dying star. The Crab Nebula is easy to spot, using a small telescope, because it is the brightest supernova in the sky.

FAST FACT Saturn's ring system is less than a mile thick but is very wide. The rings extend outward to about 260,000 miles from Saturn's surface.

The sun is far away, but it can still burn.

Even though it's so far away, the sun's light and heat allows life to exist on Earth. Because it's so hot, it's easy to get a sunburn even though it's 93 million miles away.

The sun is a very strong star.

The sun's strong gravitational pull holds Earth and the other planets in orbit in the solar system.

Solar Maze

Take a trip through the solar system, but watch out for comets and meteor showers!

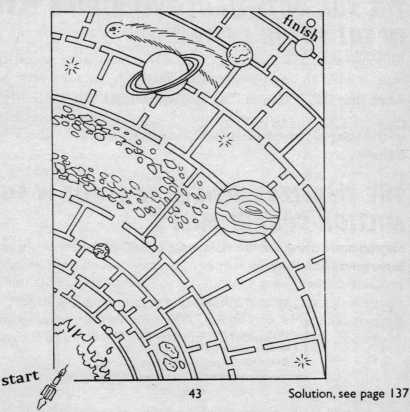

 Solution, see page 137

THE SUN IS REALLY A YELLOW DWARF!

That's what astronomers call a star like the sun because it is small but not the smallest type of star. The sun measures about 870,000 miles in diameter. There are stars that are much bigger than our sun. These stars are called red giants and supergiants. Some supergiant stars can measure about 250 million miles in diameter.

The sun is extremely important to Earth and to our solar system, but on the scale of the galaxy and the universe, the sun is just an average star. It is one of hundreds of billions of stars in our galaxy, the Milky Way, which is just one of more than 100 billion galaxies in the observable universe. The main difference between the sun and other stars is that the sun is much closer to Earth.

THE SUN OUTWEIGHS EVERYTHING ELSE IN THE SOLAR SYSTEM.

Although the sun's density is only 1.407 times that of water, its mass is 332,946 times greater than Earth's. It has a diameter of more than 865,000 miles. The sun, with a mass of $1,958 \times 10^{27}$ metric tons, represents more than 99 percent of the total mass of the solar system. The sun will exhaust its energy in about five billion years.

THE SMALLEST VISIBLE SUNSPOT IS 500 MILLION SQUARE MILES.

Sunspots are areas on the visible surface of the sun that are slightly less hot than the rest of its surface. Just to be seen by the protected naked eye, a sunspot has to have an area of 500 million square miles, or about 1/2,000th of the sun's area. The largest sunspot seen so far was about 7,000 million square miles in area. A sunspot in 1943 lasted from June to December, for 200 days.

Sunshine

Can you figure out the "sunny" word in each picture? Pick your answer from the sunny word list.

sunbelt	**sunbonnet**	**sunburst**
sunrise	**sunscreen**	**sunspot**

1._____ 2._____

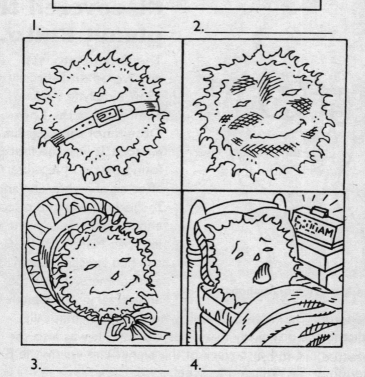

3._____ 4._____

FAST FACT How hot is it in the core. or center. of the sun? It's about 27 million degrees Fahrenheit!

Solution, see page 137

Shooting stars were first recorded in the United States of America in 1799.

The first display of shooting stars, or meteors, was observed on November 12, 1799, off the Florida Keys, by Andrew Ellicott. He reported: "The whole heaven appeared as if illuminated with sky rockets."

Clyde William Tombaugh

An American discovered the planet Pluto.

The planet Pluto was discovered on February 18, 1930, by Clyde William Tombaugh, at the Lowell Observatory, in Flagstaff, Arizona. It was the first planet found beyond Neptune. Only after careful checking and rechecking was the discovery announced—nearly one month later, on March 13, 1930. This day had special meaning for astronomers. It was the anniversary of the birth of the astronomer Dr. Percival Lowell, who had mathematically predicted the discovery many years before. It was also the 149th anniversary of the discovery of the planet Uranus by the British astronomer Sir William Herschel.

FAST FACT The tail of the Great Comet of 1843 was 105 million miles long.

The Herschels, a brother-sister team of astronomers.

The discoverers of Uranus, Sir William Herschel and his sister, Caroline, first named the planet Georgium Sidus, in honor of King George III, their patron. The name was later changed to Uranus. It was the first discovery of a planet since ancient times. Both Herschels had been musicians before entering astronomy. Caroline is the first woman to discover a comet.

Comets have been spotted in the sky for almost 2,500 years.

Approximately 2,000 comets have been observed and written about over the past 2,500 years. Halley's comet was first spotted in 467 BC. The British astronomer Edmund Halley (1656–1742) predicted that the comet would return in 1758. He was correct. It reappeared on Christmas Day, 1758, 16 years after the astronomer's death. It reappears about every 76 years.

Outer Space Matching

Can you match these outer space words with their meanings?

1. Jupiter

2. Asteroid

3. Mars

4. Comet

a) Object in the sky with a tail

b) The Red Planet

c) Small celestial body

d) Largest planet

     Solution, see page 138

EARTH IS NOT ROUND.

Earth is a globe with a bulge in the middle at the equator. It is slightly flat at the North and South Poles.

THERE ARE MORE PEOPLE NORTH OF THE EQUATOR.

Not only do most of the people on Earth live north of the equator, but there's also more land up there as well.

EARTH IS MADE UP OF LAYERS, LIKE AN ONION.

At the very heart of Earth is a core made of iron and nickel. Next there's a layer called a mantle. That's solid rock. Then there's an outer layer, called the crust, which covers Earth like a thin skin. Each layer has sublayers as well.

ALL WE KNOW ABOUT THE INSIDE OF EARTH COMES FROM EARTHQUAKES.

Researchers have drilled deep holes, such as those for oil wells, into Earth's crust. No hole has ever been drilled all the way through the crust into the mantle. Our information about inner Earth comes from studying earthquakes.

EARTH'S INNER CORE SPINS ON ITS OWN.

The inner core of Earth is solid and is made of iron and nickel. It is about 780 miles across. It is suspended in an outer core of liquid metal. It spins independently of Earth. Scientists believe that it is spinning faster than the planet itself.

Earth Uncovered

Write in the names of the different layers of Earth in the spaces provided.

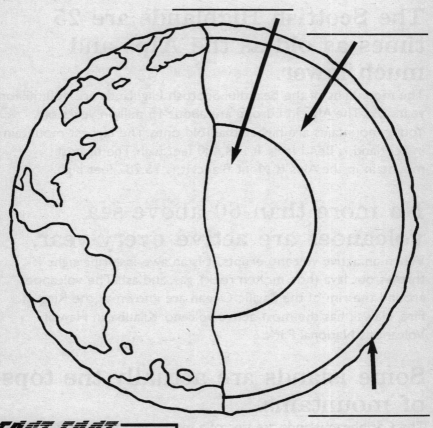

FAST FACT Nearly three quarters of Earth's surface is covered by water.

Solution, see page 138

There are earthquakes under the sea as well as on land.

The giant waves known as tsunamis ("harbor waves") are the result of earthquakes under the ocean. When you drop something in the water, you get a series of waves. This also happens when the ocean floor is tilted or offset during an earthquake.

The Scottish Highlands are 25 times as old as the Alps and much lower.

The mountains of the beautiful Scottish Highlands are 400 million years old. The Alps in Europe are about 15 million years old. Young mountains are higher than old ones. The highest mountain in Scotland is Ben Nevis. It is 4,400 feet high. The highest mountain in the Alps is Mont Blanc. It is 15,782 feet high.

No more than 60 above-sea volcanoes are active every year.

When an active volcano erupts, it is an awe-inspiring sight. It throws out lava (hot, molten rock), gas, and ash. The volcanoes around the rim of the Pacific Ocean are known as the Ring of Fire. Hawaii has the most active volcano: Kilauea, in Hawaii Volcanoes National Park.

Some islands are actually the tops of mountains.

The Caribbean islands are tips of a mountain range on the ocean floor. Many islands in the Pacific Ocean are also the tops of undersea mountains.

Mountain Mystery

To solve the Mountain Mystery, fill in the answers to the clues, one letter on each space. Then transfer the letters to the boxes below that have the same numbers. When all the boxes are filled in, you will find the answer to the Mountain Mystery. (Hint: It's a high point).

1. ___ ___ ___   2,000 pounds
   5   2   4

2 ___ ___ ___ ___ ___   poem
  7 8 9 11 10

3. ___ ___ ___ ___   silent
   1 3 12 6

☐	☐	☐	☐	☐		☐	☐	☐	☐	☐	☐	☐
1	2	3	4	5		6	7	8	9	10	11	12

FAST FACT

Of the 29 highest mountains in the world, all but two are in Asia.

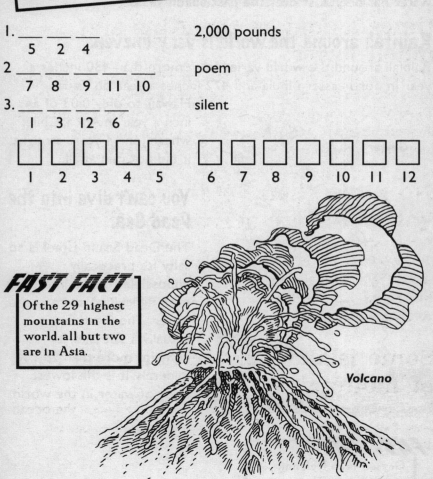

Volcano

Solution, see page 138

Rainfall includes snow.

Rainfall means all the water that falls in a given area. That includes rain, snow, hail, sleet, dew, and frost. 12 inches of snow equals one inch of rain.

Earth recycles all its water.

The planet uses and reuses all the water ever created. Very little water has been lost over the past billion years.

Rainfall around the world is very uneven.

Rainfall around the world varies from more than 430 inches a year in northeastern India and 472 inches a year on Kauai, Hawaii, to only 0.03 of an inch a year in Arica, Chile, where for 14 years straight it did not rain at all.

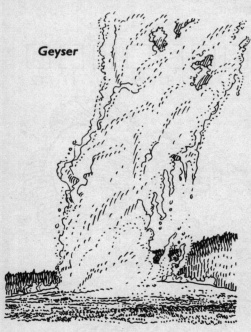

Geyser

You can't dive into the Dead Sea.

The Dead Sea in Israel is so salty it's practically impossible to dive into it. It's even difficult to swim in the water. The Dead Sea is actually a salt lake. It contains more than 25 minerals. It is the lowest body of water in the world.

FAST FACT

"Geyser" is an Icelandic word. It means "hot spring."

Homes in Iceland are heated by hot springs.

Iceland has many hot springs and geysers. Deep in the earth, water is heated by hot volcanic rock. This superheated water shoots its way to the surface as geysers. In addition to geysers, heated water comes to the surface as hot springs and boiling mud lakes. The hot water from these springs is run through pipes in many homes in Iceland to heat them.

Water Words

A little bit from each of the following water words has been pried out, leaving them high and dry. To dampen them again, take each three-letter word from the word list and place it into the correct "wet" word.

all	**bur**	**can**
ink	**owe**	**own**	**rig**

1. cloud__ __ __st

2. d__ __ __pour

3. hurri__ __ __e

4. ir__ __ __ate

5. rainf__ __ __

6. sh__ __ __r

7. spr__ __ __le

Glacier ice covers more than 10 percent of Earth's surface.

Glaciers are sheets of ice that move slowly down mountain valleys. These ice sheets can be more than 9,000 feet thick. About 80 percent of all the freshwater on Earth is frozen in glaciers.

Icebergs hide most of themselves in the water.

Fragments of ice that break off from glaciers and ice sheets are icebergs. These enormous pieces of ice float out to sea and endanger sailing ships. An iceberg that was 208 miles long and 60 miles wide (almost as large as the entire country of Belgium!) was spotted by a U.S. Coast Guard icebreaker in 1956, in the Ross Sea, Antarctica. Most of an iceberg hides below the water. Only 10 percent to 12 percent of an iceberg can be seen.

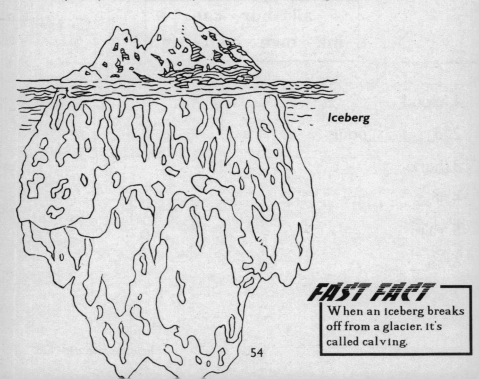

Iceberg

FAST FACT

When an iceberg breaks off from a glacier. It's called calving.

Not all lakes contain freshwater.

Some lakes contain salt water, not fresh. The Dead Sea in Israel, the Great Salt Lake in Utah, and the Caspian Sea in Russia (the world's largest inland body of water) are all salty.

The Pacific Ocean is nearly seven miles deep.

The Pacific Ocean is the world's largest ocean. It stretches from Antarctica in the south to the Bering Strait in the north. It is deeper than any other ocean, going down to 36,210 feet in the Challenger Deep of the Mariana Trench. The Challenger Deep is the deepest point on Earth. The Mariana Trench is the lowest region on Earth's surface. It's 200 miles east of the Mariana Islands in the northwest Pacific Ocean.

Change in the Weather

Change a single letter in each word in the list to make the word have something to do with things icy and frosty.

1. child

2. bold

3. solar

4. winery

5. foolish

More than 600 different species of plants live in the hottest place in the world.

Death Valley is the hottest spot in the world. However, hundreds of plants manage to live there as well as a great variety of animals. Death Valley was given its name by gold hunters of 1849 who nearly lost their lives in the heat. The summer temperatures in Death Valley shoot above 125° Fahrenheit. In 1913, a temperature of 134° Fahrenheit was recorded—the highest temperature ever recorded in the United States.

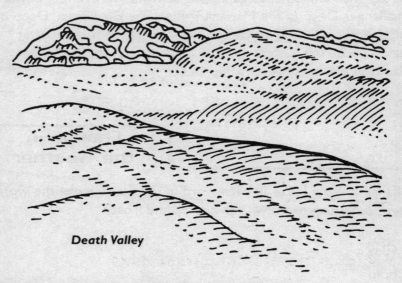

Death Valley

Whirlpools can suck down whatever is caught in them.

A whirlpool is a fast-moving swirl of water with a low place in the center. Its violent spinning can pull surrounding floating objects, such as small boats, down into the center. Whirlpools or maelstroms can be found in the oceans, rivers, and lakes. There is a famous whirlpool near Niagara Falls called the Whirlpool Rapids.

A polar sled expedition of 1,000 miles took almost 80 days to reach its goal.

A British team of explorers traveled 1,080 miles across Greenland by dogsled. The journey, from June 18 to September 5, 1934, used 49 dogs. Much of Greenland is covered by an ice sheet that is almost 5,000 feet thick.

FAST FACT Death Valley is the lowest point in the Western Hemisphere.

Geographic Goofs

Do you know the answers to these tricky questions?

1. Where's the ATM in Greenland?

2. How do Death Valley cops chase their quarry?

3. What kind of fishing equipment do you use in a whirlpool?

The winter weather on the West Coast is usually more moderate and warmer than on the East Coast.

Because prevailing winds in North America move from west to east, the West Coast gets its weather from the Pacific Ocean. While it does get stormy out in the Pacific, it doesn't happen too often.

Australia got its name because it was unknown.

Australia was not known to the Western world for many centuries. However, ancient scholars believed that a land just had to be there, to balance the lands of Europe and Asia. They called this imaginary place Terra Australis Incognita, or a "Great Unknown Southland." On old maps it appeared as a mysterious, uncharted region. When it was finally discovered, it had its name already waiting for it: Terra Australis, which became Australia.

Australia is either the smallest continent or the largest island.

Australia is a land of strange facts. It has been called the largest island in the world and the smallest continent. It is also the sixth-largest country in the world. Because it is not connected to any other landmasses, it has plant and animal life unlike any other place on Earth.

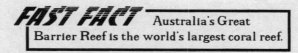

FAST FACT Australia's Great Barrier Reef is the world's largest coral reef.

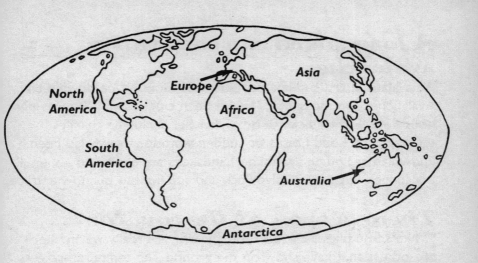

Australian Words

How many words can you make out of the word **AUSTRALIA**? Can you make 10?

_____   _____

_____   _____

_____   _____

_____   _____

_____   _____

    Solution, see page 139

A loud sound can cause an avalanche.

An avalanche is a sudden movement of snow or ice down a cliff. Avalanches can move fast. They've been clocked at 100 miles per hour. Several things can cause avalanches, including changes in temperature. Loud noises or sudden vibrations have also been known to set off an avalanche. Landslides are similar to avalanches, but they involve rock and soil instead of snow and ice.

There is snow at the equator.

While some places close to the equator are really warm, there are others that have snow on the ground. The temperature gets lower the higher you climb. The higher the altitude, the colder it gets, no matter where you are. So the highest mountain in Africa, Mt. Kilimanjaro, which lies three degrees south of the equator, has a crown of snow all year round.

The deepest lake in the world is fed by 300 rivers.

Lake Baikal, in Siberia, is the deepest lake in the world. It is 5,371 feet deep. The third-largest lake in Asia and the eighth largest in the world, it is more than 12,000 square miles in size. More than 300 rivers flow into it.

FAST FACT Lake Baikal holds approximately 20 percent of all Earth's fresh surface water.

Keeping Cool at the Equator

Some folks living at the equator want to keep cool by climbing Mt. Kilimanjaro. Can you show them the way up?

Solution, see page 139

Some things can spontaneously burst into flame.

When heat builds up internally in certain piled-up materials, such as oil-soaked rags, they can burst into flame. This is called spontaneous combustion.

Water running down a drain at the equator does not swirl in any direction.

Water running down a drain in the Northern Hemisphere swirls counterclockwise (opposite the usual direction that a clock's hands move). Water running down a drain in the Southern Hemisphere swirls clockwise. This is called the Coriolis effect. As a result of Earth's rotation, moving objects (air currents, moving water, even long-range projectiles) are pushed to one side. At the equator, this effect doesn't apply. Water running down a drain will run straight down.

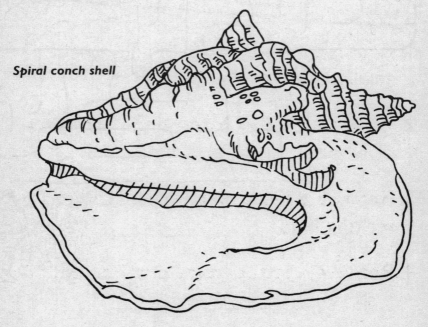

Spiral conch shell

The sounds heard in a seashell are not imaginary.

If you hold a seashell up to your ear, you will hear sounds. These are actually soft sounds of your surroundings, such as the beach, which have been amplified, or made louder, by the seashell's cavity.

FAST FACT The equator passes through 13 countries.

Remove the Shell

Remove one letter from a word to make another word without rearranging any letters.

1. Remove a letter from "shell" to get a salesman's routine. _____

2. Remove a letter from "drain" to get a downpour. _____

3. Remove a letter from "sink" to get writing fluid. _____

4. Remove a letter from "drag" to get a shred. _____

Solution, see page 139

Liquid water is denser than ice.

Liquid water decreases in density as it freezes. That means more molecules occupy the same amount of space in liquid water than in ice. That's why ice can float on top of liquid water.

Medieval alchemists believed there was a substance that could change things into gold.

Alchemist

They called this substance a philosopher's stone. In addition to turning things into gold, it supposedly had the power of curing all injuries and diseases. It was all fantasy. The imaginary philosopher's stone never existed.

Certain metals are considered "noble."

The noble metals are gold, silver, mercury, and the platinum group (platinum, iridium, palladium, rhodium, ruthenium, and osmium). What makes them "noble" is the fact that they don't rust easily and can resist chemical reaction. Being a noble metal has nothing to do with being a precious metal, even though gold, silver, and platinum fit into both groups.

There are two elements that are liquid at room temperature.

Mercury, or quicksilver, is the element most people know as being liquid at room temperature. Room temperature is defined as 68° to 70° Fahrenheit. But there's another element, bromine, that is also liquid at room temperature. Two other elements—gallium and cesium—turn liquid just above room temperature. Gallium melts at 85.6° Fahrenheit and cesium melts at 83° Fahrenheit.

This rare gas isn't rare at all.

Helium is called a rare gas, because it is rarefied—it has very low density. It's found in small amounts in Earth's atmosphere and in some substances. But in the universe, it's the second-most abundant element after hydrogen.

FAST FACT The two elements that are liquid at room temperature have their own special colors. Mercury is silvery while bromine is dark red.

March of the Nobles

Put the noble metals to the test. Can you answer these tricky questions about gold and its fellow metals?

1. Add the word "quick" to one noble metal to get another.

2. Find the metal that's hiding in a noble metal.

3. Which noble metal is the friendliest?

4. Find the girl in a noble metal.

Solution, see page 139

The most useful chemical in the world makes your french fries taste better.

It's salt—good old sodium chloride. Salt has more than 14,000 different uses. It is used in larger quantities and in many more ways than any other known chemical.

A man named Fahrenheit invented the thermometer.

Daniel Fahrenheit gave his name to the thing he invented—the thermometer. In 1713, he developed a thermometer that had two fixed points: The melting point of ice and the body heat of a healthy person. Melting ice was set at 32 degrees and the heat of a person at 96 degrees, which was later changed to 98.6 degrees.

One standard temperature scale accidentally reversed the freezing and boiling points.

In 1742, Anders Celsius told the world that water froze at 100 degrees centigrade, and it boiled at 0 degrees. It's the exact opposite, of course. Another scientist, Carolus Linnaeus, later fixed the mistake, but we still call that particular temperature scale after Celsius, not Linnaeus.

Ampere, volt, and watt were real

FAST FACT The Celsius scale is also called the centigrade scale.

people before they became electrical units.

André-Marie Ampère (1775–1836) gave his name to the unit of electric current we call the ampere, or amp. He was a French physicist.

The volt is named for Alessandro Volta (1745–1827), an Italian scientist who built the first modern battery.

Alessandro Volta

We measure electric power in watts, which remembers James Watt (1736–1819), the Scottish inventor of the steam engine.

Shocking Couples

Is an electric current light an amp lamp? Turn on the switch for some more rhymes. Just add the missing word for a rhyme.

1. A boat ride's electrical safety devices   cruise's _____

2. Where NASA lights up   rocket _____

3. Cable purchaser   _____ buyer

4. Unlit electric arc   dark _____

Solution, see page 139

Everybody belongs to a blood group.

There are four blood groups: A, B, AB, and O. Everyone belongs to one of them.

Coal miners are afraid of "damp."

Damp is any kind of dangerous gas in a mine. White damp is another name for the poisonous gas carbon monoxide. The explosive methane, or marsh gas, is called firedamp. When firedamp explodes, it forms the suffocating gas chokedamp. Well-ventilated mines help prevent this from happening.

The glass in a movie is actually candy.

Most of the breakable glass that's used on a movie set is really sweet stuff. It's boiled sugar that is dripped out onto flat panels and allowed to harden. When it breaks during a fake fight, for instance, nobody gets hurt.

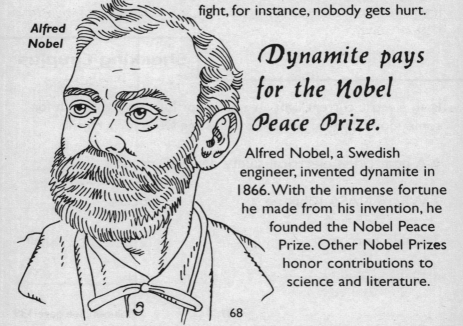

Alfred Nobel

Dynamite pays for the Nobel Peace Prize.

Alfred Nobel, a Swedish engineer, invented dynamite in 1866. With the immense fortune he made from his invention, he founded the Nobel Peace Prize. Other Nobel Prizes honor contributions to science and literature.

There was only one plastic until 1906.

Celluloid, a hard and flexible transparent material, was the only plastic made until 1906. It was used to make combs, buttons, and movie film. Then, in 1906, Bakelite, another early plastic, was invented and soon took away celluloid's monopoly. Since then, plastics such as rayon and nylon have been invented.

FAST FACT Coal miners in the 1800s used canaries to test for carbon monoxide. If the canary died. the miners knew they needed to move to fresh air.

A Plastic Puzzler

Somebody melted down the plastics. It's up to you to return them to their former state. Each one is lacking a special ingredient. Add the special ingredient, and you'll have the plastics back to normal.

a) __ __ __ __ lite

b) __ __ __ __ uloid

c) __ __ __ on

d) __ __ __ tate

Special Ingredients
ace
bake
cell
ray

Some petroleum now comes from plants.

Two plants, the gopher plant and the petroleum nut, supply diesel fuel substitutes. The available quantities are still small, however.

The first service station was French.

In December 1895, Monsieur A. Barol of Bordeaux, France, opened the world's first service station. He offered car repair, parking, and oil and gas ("motor spirit"). We still use the French word for service station—garage. The first American garage was opened in Boston, Massachusetts, on May 24, 1899. It was advertised as "a stable for renting, sale, storage, and repair of motor vehicles."

An early 1900s service station

FAST FACT In 1912. a gas station opened in Memphis. Tennessee. It had 13 pumps and a maid who served ice water to thirsty drivers.

Releasing toy balloons into the air can be dangerous.

If a rubber balloon floats over and lands in water, it can sometimes be mistaken for food by sea animals and be eaten. Because the animals cannot digest it, the balloon can hurt them. Foil balloons sometimes get caught in electric transmission wires and cause power outages.

A lot of newspapers need to be recycled to save a tree.

To save a single tree, a stack of newspapers four feet high has to be recycled. That's the amount of newspaper produced by a 35-foot-high tree. One ton of recycled paper saves 17 trees.

Oil Challenge

Read the clues and then fill in each blank to find the correct "oil" word or phrase.

1. Type of art   oil _____

2. Goes with vinegar   _____ oil

3. Edmonton hockey team   oil____

4. Work late   _____ ___ _____ oil

5. Baloney   _____ oil

Solution, see page 139

A simple fern has the largest number of chromosomes.

The fern species *Ophioglossum reticulatum* has the most chromosomes—1,260, or 630 pairs. Humans have 46, or 23 pairs. Dogs have 78, or 39 pairs.

There are now five kingdoms of living things.

Biologists once divided all living things into two kingdoms: animal and plant. But there were living things that didn't fit into either category. Today, scientists put living things into one of the following five kingdoms:

Monera — Includes bacteria and blue-green algae.

Protista — Includes diatoms, slime molds, protozoa, and euglena.

Fungi — Includes mushrooms, yeasts, and molds.

Plantae — Includes multicelled plant life.

Animalia — Includes multicelled animal life.

Protozoa

Bacteria exist that can eat through stone.

Certain microbes actually eat stone. Some are helpful, some are not. Members of the *Thiobacillus* genus damage buildings, sculptures, and monuments. These bacteria can turn hard marble into soft, crumbly plaster. On the other hand, other bacteria of the same genus may be useful. They manufacture sulfuric acid, which helps remove copper from ore. This is much more environmentally friendly than the costly industrial methods commonly used today.

Lawn clippings should be left on the grass after mowing.

Nitrogen, phosphorus, and potassium in lawn clippings feed the new grass, so less fertilizer is needed. Rather than dumping old clippings in the trash, leaving lawn clippings on the grass cuts down the amount of waste added to landfills.

Matching

Match each living being with its proper kingdom.

1. Monera ___
2. Protista ___
3. Fungi ___
4. Plantae ___
5. Animalia ___

a. bacteria

b. cow

c. mushroom

d. protozoa

e. rose

Solution, see page 140

Potatoes, tomatoes, and eggplants are in the same family as deadly nightshade.

Three popular and non-poisonous vegetables—potatoes, tomatoes, and eggplants—are in the same family as the poisonous deadly nightshade. There are about 2,600 species of nightshade plants.

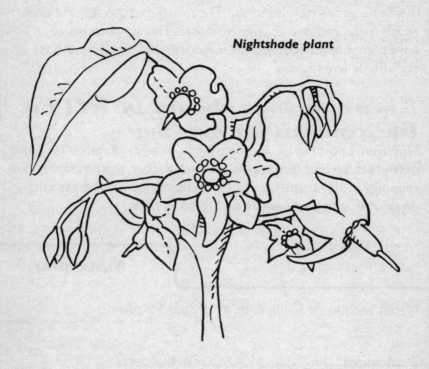

Nightshade plant

FAST FACT President Thomas Jefferson. who'd lived in France. gets credited for bringing french fries to the U.S. He had them served at the White House.

The nautical mile has nothing to do with the land mile.

While the two kinds of miles both measure distances, they are different standards. The land mile, or statute mile, is 5,280 feet. The word "mile" refers to the distance covered in a thousand paces by the Roman army. The nautical mile is based on the circumference of Earth and is used at sea.

1 nautical mile = 1.1508 statute miles, or 6,076 feet.
1 statute mile = 0.868976 nautical miles, or 5,280 feet.

A knot is one nautical mile per hour. It is a measure of speed, not distance.

Three countries have not converted to the metric system.

Only three countries have not formally converted to the metric system. They are Myanmar (formerly Burma), Liberia, and the United States. Thomas Jefferson (1743–1826) suggested that the United States convert to the metric system in 1790. We decided not to because our major trading partner at the time, Great Britain, wasn't using the system. In 1965, Great Britain switched to the metric system, but we still have not.

Metric Match

From the list of metric units below, match each one with the correct non-metric unit. For example, an ounce might go with a gram.

1. kilometer   a. mile

2. liter   b. inch

3. centimeter   c. quart

Daylight saving time is not observed in some parts of the United States.

There are certain areas of the United States that are exempt from daylight saving time. They are Arizona, Hawaii, Puerto Rico, the U.S. Virgin Islands, and American Samoa. Parts of Indiana are exempt as well.

The whole world is divided into time zones.

The world is covered by 24 standard time zones, one for each hour of the day.

The hands on a clock go clockwise because of the sun's movements.

Before clocks were invented, man used sundials to keep track of the time. The shadow of the sundial moves in a clockwise direction in the Northern Hemisphere. Clockmakers copied this movement.

Grandfather clocks today have nothing to do with grandfathers.

Grandfather clocks should really be called long-case clocks. A popular song of the 1800s, "My Grandfather's Clock," gave the tall clock a new name, which has been used ever since. The song was written by Henry Work around 1875. The song was very popular in the United States.

FAST FACT China stretches across five time zones, but doesn't change its time. Instead of moving one hour for each time zone, China keeps the same time for all five time zones.

Watch the Maze

Can you make your way through this grandfather clock maze?

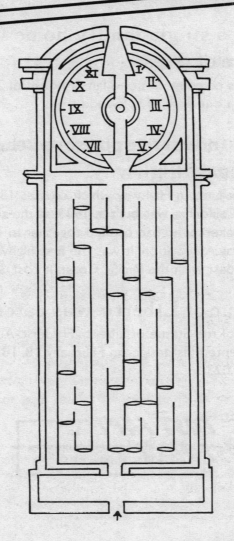

Solution, see page 140

The first alarm clock rang only at 4 AM.

The first alarm clock was made by Levi Hutchins of Concord, New Hampshire, in 1787. It was 29 inches high and 14 inches wide. It had a pine case and a mirror in the door. The alarm would sound only at 4 in the morning and could not be changed.

Building a single-family home will use up an acre of trees.

By the time it's completed, a one-family house of 2,000 square feet will use up one acre of softwood trees.

The auto industry sponsored the first coast-to-coast highway.

The 3,389-mile Lincoln Highway, which crosses 13 states, from New York to California, was built in 1923, at the suggestion of a group of carmakers who had banded together in 1913 as the Lincoln Highway Association. It was the first highway connecting the Atlantic Coast with the Pacific Coast. It cost $10,000,000.

The Statue of Liberty was patented.

The designer of the Statue of Liberty, Frédéric-Auguste Bartholdi, patented his design on February 18, 1879 (U.S. Design Patent No. 11,023).

FAST FACT In 1925. the Lincoln Highway became U.S. Route 30.

The charge to ride the first Ferris wheel was 50 cents.

In 1893, steel engineer George Washington Gale Ferris built the first Ferris wheel. The highest point of the wheel was 264 feet. It was a feature of the midway at the 1893 Columbian Exposition in Chicago, Illinois. The 20-minute ride cost $0.50, or about $7.00 in today's money. Ferris made a profit of more than a million dollars.

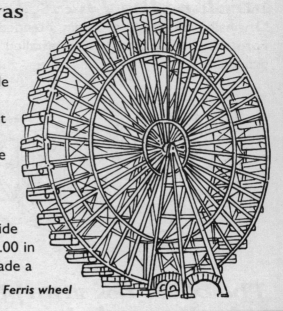

Ferris wheel

On the Road

See how many road words you can find from the list. Look down and across.

Word list: highway, street, avenue, lane

H	I	G	H	W	A	Y	X
T	D	Z	M	R	V	Q	B
M	J	L	A	N	E	T	A
A	I	E	O	D	N	Z	U
E	B	X	T	U	U	P	L
A	S	T	R	E	E	T	C

Solution, see page 140

The Wright brothers named their airplane the *Flyer*.

Originally, the Wright brothers intended the *Flyer* to be a glider. For its first flight, though, they installed a small motor and two propellers.

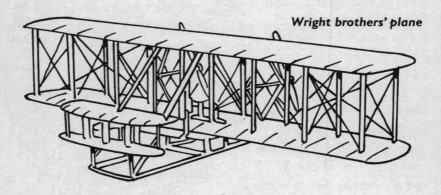

Wright brothers' plane

The black box in airplanes is actually painted orange.

Flight data recorders (FDRs) and cockpit voice recorders (CVRs) are used to investigate the cause of an aviation accident. The crash-proof black boxes, which are a bright orange, hold vital information, including the airplane's speed and altitude, and recordings of conversations in the cockpit.

Radio station call letters were assigned by location.

With a few exceptions, most radio stations located west of the Mississippi were assigned call letters beginning with the letter K. Radio stations east of the Mississippi were usually given call letters starting with the letter W.

The inventor of modern television got his idea while plowing a field.

Philo T. Farnsworth (1906–1971) is now generally credited with inventing television. His idea for a scanning camera was an important part of television. He got the idea when he was plowing a field in Idaho. He told his high school science teacher about his idea, and was encouraged in his work. Farnsworth also invented an early electron microscope. He held more than 150 patents.

TV Mystery

Match each number to the letter in the code to find the television words.

A	B	C	D	E	F	G	H	I	J	K	L	M
1	2	3	4	5	6	7	8	9	10	11	12	13
N	O	P	Q	R	S	T	U	V	W	X	Y	Z
14	15	16	17	18	19	20	21	22	23	24	25	26

a) 3 8 1 14 14 5 12 _____

b) 3 1 2 12 5 _____

c) 19 9 20 3 15 13 _____

d) 19 5 19 1 13 5   19 20 18 5 5 20 _____

FAST FACT The first televised major-league baseball games were a double-header between the Cincinnati Reds and the Brooklyn Dodgers on August 26, 1939.

The fax machine was invented in 1843, in Scotland.

A Scottish clockmaker, Alexander Bain (1818–1903), invented the first facsimile, or "fax," machine in 1843. It was a very complicated invention that required pendulums in order to work!

The first electronic computer was a code-breaking machine.

In order to crack the secret German military codes during World War II, British scientists developed the world's first programmable electronic computer in 1943. The British never told anyone about it until many years after the war.

Admiral Grace Hopper

An admiral in the U.S. Navy was the first modern computer programmer.

Although simple programming had been around since the 1800s, the first modern programmer was Admiral Grace Murray Hopper, USN (1906–1992). She was a high-ranking officer in the U.S. Navy and a brilliant computer scientist. Admiral Hopper developed the first compiler (a type of advanced computer program). She also invented an early version of the programming language COBOL (common business oriented language).

The zero was an invention of mathematicians in India.

Until mathematicians in India came up with the concept of zero, it was very hard to do more than very simple arithmetic. For instance, the Romans couldn't show the answer for VIII − VIII ($8 - 8 = 0$)! They had no symbol to represent zero. In fact, for many years, there was no zero in arithmetic! Then Arab merchants brought the zero to Europe. All of a sudden it became easier to do arithmetic.

Computer Quiz

Fill in the missing letter to complete each computer term.

1. mo___se

2. prog___am

3. ke___board

4. ha___d drive

5. pi___el

FAST FACT Admiral Grace Hopper was the first to use the word "bug" to mean a programming problem or error. Her computer stopped working and she poked around to find a little beetle had gotten inside. She pulled it out and said. "All I had to do was de-bug the computer!"

The first air bags were developed for use in space capsules.

In 1953, the first air bag was invented. It was originally intended to be used in space capsules to protect astronauts from injury. However, it was not used for that purpose. Several years later, carmakers had it redesigned for use in automobiles.

People have an internal biological clock.

The biological clock controls the natural rhythms of life, including when to get up or when to get hungry. When you get sleepy, your biological clock is telling you that your body is tired. Some people like to wake up early. Others like to go to bed early. It's their biological clock at work. Jet lag occurs when we change the rhythms of our bodies on a long airplane flight and our internal clock gets mixed up. Our bodies don't know what time it is!

Archaeologists use carbon to date the fossils they find.

Carbon dating is a way of figuring out the age of very old things. It helps establish the age of fossils and even ancient pottery or weapons. The amount of carbon found in artifacts, such as pottery or fossils, helps archaeologists determine the age of the object.

FAST FACT Plants also have internal clocks that tell them when to open and close their petals.

A Polish scientist proved that Earth orbits around the sun.

Before the work of Polish astronomer Nicolaus Copernicus (1473–1543) in 1540, people believed that the sun rotated around Earth. But the great astronomer proved that Earth rotates on its axis, and revolves around the sun, along with all the other planets in the solar system.

A husband-and-wife team discovered radium.

The radioactive element called radium was discovered and given its name by Pierre and Marie Curie in 1898. They were awarded the Nobel Prize in Physics in 1903. Marie Curie was also awarded the Nobel Prize for Chemistry in 1911 for her work with radioactivity.

Marie Curie

Which One Does Not Belong?

In each line below, one of the four terms does not belong with the others. Circle the one that does not fit.

1. radium, Mr. & Mrs. Curie, air bag, Nobel Prize
2. Copernicus, Earth, sun, orbit, man in moon
3. stale bread, carbon dating, fossils, archaeology

Solution, see page 140

The average human body contains 47 elements, including gold.

In addition to oxygen, hydrogen, carbon, calcium, and 42 other elements, the human body has a hint of gold (0.00034 ounces).

There are 50 trillion cells in the human body.

The cell is the basic unit of life. The human body has more than 200 different kinds of cells. Human cells vary in size from small red blood cells that measure 0.00003 inch to liver cells that are 10 times larger. About 10,000 human cells can fit on the head of a pin.

We take 600 million breaths in an average lifetime.

We breathe in 13 pints of air every minute. This air contains nitrogen, oxygen, and carbon dioxide. The air we breathe out contains almost 100 times more carbon dioxide than we take in.

Hiccups can usually be stopped by holding the breath.

Hiccups, or hiccoughs, are caused by a sudden, involuntary contraction of the diaphragm (the muscular partition separating the chest and abdominal cavities). This causes air to be suddenly inhaled. As the air rushes to the lungs, a valve at the opening (glottis) into the windpipe snaps shut to keep too much air from getting into lungs. The vocal cords rapidly close, producing the sharp "hic" sound. Hiccups may be stopped by holding one's breath or breathing in and out of a paper bag.

FAST FACT Snoring occurs when air from the lungs causes a small piece of tissue at the back of the throat. the uvula. to vibrate. The result is a rough. hoarse sound.

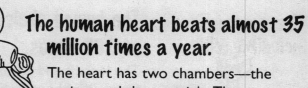

The human heart beats almost 35 million times a year.

The heart has two chambers—the atrium and the ventricle. These contract and relax every 0.8 seconds, sending out almost three fluid ounces of blood with every beat.

Human heart

About the Body

In this game, if you take a letter away from the name of a body part, you'll get another word.

1. Remove a letter from "heart" to get a word that means to listen.
2. Remove a letter from "bone" to get an individual.
3. Remove a letter from "face" to get a top pilot.
4. Remove a letter from "hand" to get a plus.
5. Remove a letter from "heel" to get a fish.
6. Remove a letter from "skin" to get a relative.
7. Remove a letter from "brain" to get precipitation.
8. Remove a letter from "gland" to get territory.
9. Remove a letter from "spine" to get a word that means to whirl.
10. Remove a letter from "liver" to get a word that means to be active.
11. Remove a letter from "thigh" to get elevated.
12. Remove a letter from "pelvis" to get the "king of rock 'n' roll."

Solution, see page 140

The human skeleton is made up of 206 bones.

The longest and strongest bone is the femur (thighbone), which in some people can be 20 inches long and one inch wide. The smallest bone, the stapes, or stirrup bone, is one of three tiny bones buried within the middle ear. It is less than the size of a rice grain. More than 300 bones are present in an infant, several of which fuse as the infant matures.

While bone seems to be just a hard substance, it is really made of both living and non-living material. It contains bone cells, blood vessels, and fat cells. Part of bone is made up of water and minerals.

Jogging and climbing stairs use about the same amount of energy.

Swimming uses about 12 times as much energy as staying in bed. Standing uses twice as much energy as staying in bed.

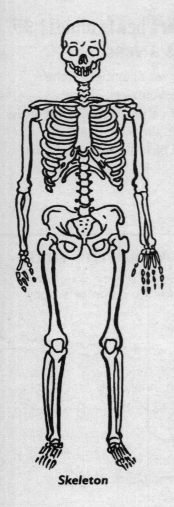

Skeleton

Teeth are harder than bone.

The enamel that protects the surface of the tooth is the hardest substance in the body.

The human body has more than 600 different voluntary muscles.

Voluntary muscles are also called skeletal muscles because they move the bones. Voluntary muscles are controlled by the brain. They do not act on their own the way the heart does.

FAST FACT "Skeleton" means "dried up" in Greek.

Hidden Anatomy

Can you see the parts of the body hidden in these sentences? Try to find hidden words for body parts in letters reading from left to right.

1. When a golfer on this fairway yells, "Fore," head for the hills.

2. The bird-watcher found a flamingo, a heron, a gull, etc.

3. Now that I have your ear, drum it into your head that you must arrive on time.

4. So far we've moved half a ton. Silt and rock get moved next.

Solution, see page 141

Hair and fingernails are made of the same substance.

Hair and fingernails are both made out of keratin, a skin protein. The horn of the rhinoceros is composed of keratin, which is also found in the hooves and claws of animals.

Hair color is due to a special pigment.

The color of hair is caused by melanin. Melanin is also the chemical that causes the variations in the color of human skin. When melanin is no longer produced as the result of aging, white or gray hair appears.

Cutting hair doesn't hurt because hair is dead.

While hair is dead, it will hurt if you try to pull it out by its roots, because the roots are alive.

We get goose bumps to keep us warm.

Certain muscles called hair erectors make hair stand up straight and cause goose bumps when it's cold. This is to trap warmth. We also get goose bumps at times of fright or excitement.

Doctors can "read" fingernails to diagnose illnesses.

Doctors are able to identify certain health problems just by looking at fingernails. The shape, color, and pattern of fingernails can reveal possible poisoning and heart disease, for instance.

The brain has 15 billion nerve cells and uses one-fourth of the body's blood supply.

Each nerve cell is connected to 25,000 other cells. Nerve signals move along at more than 250 miles per hour.

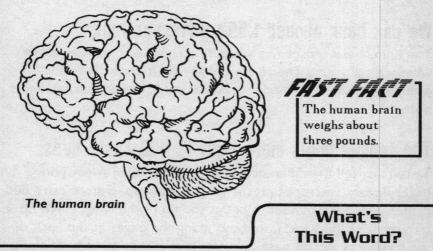

FAST FACT

The human brain weighs about three pounds.

The human brain

What's This Word?

Can you identify these words from the clues given? Hint: some of the answers are in your mirror!

1. This four-letter word starts with H and ends with R, and is our "fur."

2. This five-letter word starts with S and ends with P, and means the skin of the head.

3. This seven-letter word starts with K and ends with N, and means a skin protein.

4. This five-letter word starts with B and ends with D, and means facial hair.

Solution, see page 141

Your eyes blink about 15 times a minute.

Most of the time, blinking is done to wash away particles and keep the eyes moist with tears. Most tears are just drained away into the nose. However, crying produces tears too fast to be drained away, and that's why we will see them as teardrops rolling down the cheeks.

We can hear almost 1,500 different tones.

The human ear senses tiny vibrations. These tiny vibrations are what we call sound. The rustle of leaves (15 decibels) is one-eighth the sound of thunder (120 decibels). The human ear hears both.

The tongue holds more than 10,000 taste buds.

Taste buds tell the difference between sour, salty, sweet, and bitter flavors. Each spot on the tongue has a specialized taste bud center. We detect sweet things at the tip of the tongue. We taste bitterness at the back. Taste buds along the edges at the back of the tongue taste sourness. Saltiness is tasted by taste buds along the sides of the front. All these taste buds last for only a week before the body renews them.

People can detect about 3,200 different odors.

By detecting even the slightest hint of certain chemicals in the air, our sense of smell helps us identify different aromas. We're born with a very acute sense of smell, which fades with age.

FAST FACT When you have a cold. you lose your sense of taste. That's because your nose is stuffed. Both the nose and tongue have taste and smell cells.

A Pair of Ears

Can you find the two ears that are exactly alike?

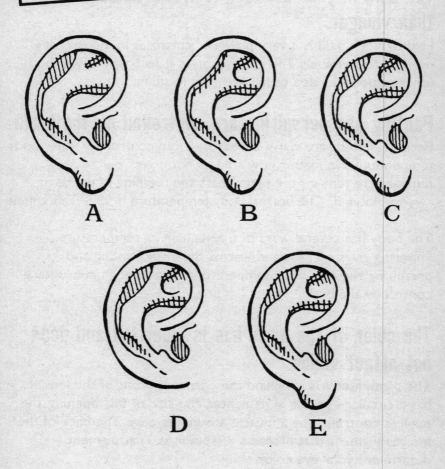

A   B   C

D   E

Solution, see page 141

The skin is the body's largest organ.

The skin takes up an average area of 20 square feet on a man, and 17 square feet on a woman. Skin renews itself all the time. It takes about a month for new tissues to replace old skin. The body sheds more than 40 pounds of skin over a lifetime.

The acid in your stomach is 1,000 times stronger than vinegar.

Hydrochloric acid is a very powerful chemical. In industry, it is used to clean metals. The stomach uses it to break down food for digestion and also to kill germs in food.

Panting and perspiring are controlled by the brain.

Because humans are warm-blooded, we can control our inner body temperature. No matter how cold or hot it gets, our body temperature remains the same. That's the meaning of the term "warm-blooded." The normal body temperature is 98.6° Fahrenheit.

The body has several ways of maintaining its temperature. Shivering gives off heat and warms the body. Panting and perspiring regulate body temperature, too, through involuntary control by the brain.

The color of the eye's iris is inherited and does not affect vision.

The pigmented iris is behind the cornea in front of the lens. It has a circular opening in its center. The size of this opening, the pupil, is controlled by a muscle around its edge. The back of the iris has pigment that protects it from light. That pigment determines your eye color.

The Eye Game

Can you name the parts of the eye?

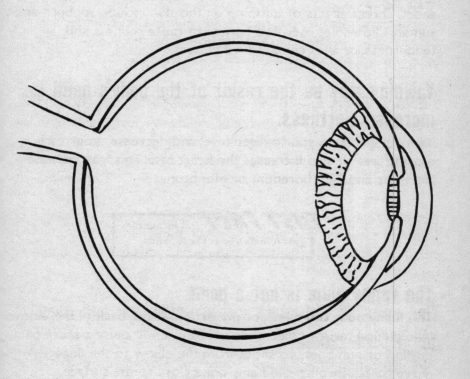

FAST FACT Dead skin makes up most household dust.

Solution, see page 141

Nine out of 10 people are right-handed.

Approximately 90 percent of the human population is predominantly right-handed. A few others are strongly left-handed, and some people are left-handed for some activities and right-handed for others. These people are called ambidextrous.

You can get sunburned on a cloudy day.

The sun still shines on a cloudy day, even though you might not see it. Direct effects of sunshine on the skin include sunburn and suntan. Ultraviolet radiation burns can cause redness and tenderness, or they can produce blisters.

Yawning may be the result of the body's need to increase alertness.

Yawning increases your oxygen level and decreases your carbon dioxide level. It also increases the heart rate. This may increase alertness and fight boredom or monotony.

FAST FACT The average yawn lasts about six seconds.

The funny bone is not a bone.

The funny bone is a bump, or projection, at the back of the elbow. Its technical term is "olecranon." Hitting it will cause a sharp pain, tingling, or numbness to shoot from the elbow to the fingers. A nerve passes through the funny bone close to the surface. Because it doesn't have much protection, hitting it can be painful.

A Day at the Beach

Look at this picture of sunbathers at the beach. Circle all the things that are wrong with the picture.

Of the seven wonders of the ancient world, only one still remains.

The ancient world boasted seven man-made wonders that travelers from all over visited. These included the Hanging Gardens of Babylon, built in the sixth century BC by King Nebuchadnezzar. The 40-foot-high ivory-and-gold statue of Zeus was erected around the fifth century BC in Olympia, Greece. The 105-foot-high Colossus of Rhodes was built around 280 BC. The Temple of Artemis, which took 120 years to build, in Ephesus, Greece, was dedicated in 430 BC. The 440-foot-high Lighthouse (Pharos) of Alexandria, was built in 280 BC, in the harbor of Alexandria, Egypt. The Mausoleum at Halicarnassus was built in 350 BC, in Turkey.

The only remaining ancient wonder of the world is the Great Pyramid, on the West Bank of the Nile River at Giza, Egypt, built around 2580 BC.

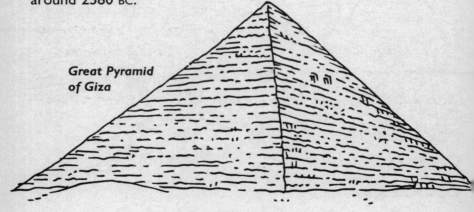

Great Pyramid of Giza

FAST FACT The first time the word "museum" appeared in English was as part of the name of the Ashmolean Museum in 1683.

The horse was domesticated around 4000 BC.

Six thousand years ago, in central Asia and Persia, horses became the partners of human beings, as beasts of burden, military chargers, modes of transportation, and in games such as early polo. Today, we have breeds as diverse as the Shetland, Percheron, Appaloosa, Clydesdale, Morgan, and Arabian.

The oldest museum in the world is in England.

The Ashmolean Museum in Oxford, England, was the first natural history museum in the world. It was established in 1683, and was based on the collections of the gardener to King Charles I.

The first wheels were solid.

The earliest known wheels were constructed in ancient Mesopotamia. They date from about 3500 to 3000 BC. These wheels were solid wooden disks.

Wild Horses

Unscramble the breeds and you'll have some mighty fine horses.

1. LAOPASAPO

2. BARIANA

3. LADCELSEDY

4. NOGRAM

5. CHEEPNORR

6. THELSAND

The alphabet comes from the Phoenicians.

A seafaring people who lived on the eastern shore of the
Mediterranean Sea invented the alphabet. These people were the
Phoenicians, and they developed the alphabet more than 3,500
years ago. Their invention spread around the world, and all
alphabets owe their beginnings to this first alphabet. A few
languages, like Chinese and Japanese, use a different type of
writing system.

The first books were clay tablets.

Sumerians, Babylonians, and other peoples of ancient
Mesopotamia (modern-day Iraq) kept their records on clay
tablets. The ancient Egyptians, Greeks, and Romans used book
rolls, or scrolls. These were made of papyrus, a material like
paper. Sheets of papyrus were formed into a continuous strip and
rolled around a stick. Scrolls are still used in Jewish synagogues.

The pharaohs of Egypt were worshiped as gods.

The kings of Egypt were called pharaohs. In Egyptian, "pharaoh"
means "great house," referring to the king's palace. Pharaohs
claimed to be descended from the god Horus, the god of light
and the sun.

The oldest game in the world is backgammon.

Backgammon is the oldest game in recorded history. A 5,000-
year-old backgammon board was found in ancient Ur, in Iraq.
Backgammon was also popular in China, India, Persia, Egypt,
Greece, and Rome.

FAST FACT Backgammon
boards from 1500 BC have been
found in Egyptian tombs.

Egyptians built the first sailing ships in 3000 BC.

To navigate upstream on the Nile River, early Egyptians built the first sailing ships. The vessels had sails hung between two masts.

Egyptian sailing ship

Writing System

The clues tell you what the blank words are. Just fill in the missing letters. The shaded letters will tell you what you are doing right now. We left a few letters to help you along.

1. These are found in books.   W _ _ _ _

2. They used clay tablets   _ G _ _ _ _ _ _ _ _

3. Named for the first two letters   _ _ _ _ _ _ _ _

4. Useful word book   _ _ _ _ _ _ _ _ _ Y

5. Gave us the ABCs   P _ _ _ _ _ _ _ _ _ _ _

6. What you do with pages   _ U _ _

7. Communicating   _ _ _ _ _ _ G

Mystery Word _ _ _ _ _ _ _ _

Solution, see page 141

The Chinese invented agriculture, the compass, gunpowder, porcelain, and paper.

In about 10,000 BC, people in China began developing agriculture. By 1500 BC the Chinese had invented the compass, gunpowder, silk, porcelain, and paper.

Bachelors over the age of 30 were not allowed to vote in ancient Sparta.

The ancient Greek country of Sparta required men to marry by the age of 30. If they did not, they lost the right to vote.

Candidates for office in ancient Rome wore white togas.

If you ran for office in ancient Rome, you were required to wear a white toga. This was a sort of a campaign poster announcing your candidacy. In fact, the word "candidate" itself comes from a Latin word meaning "white."

Ancient civilizations were usually built on top of earlier ones.

In the Middle East, ancient houses were built of adobe-like brick. These mud brick houses usually lasted no more than 75 years. When they fell apart, new houses were simply built on top of the old ones. This could go on for thousands of years. That's why archaeologists often find entire civilizations built in layers, one on top of the other.

FAST FACT Ancient Greeks believed that hot baths made people weak.

The first known dentist practiced in 3000 BC.

Egyptian dentist Hesi-Re used herbs, spices, animal parts, and magic spells to treat toothaches and swollen gums.

A-Mazing Find

Can you find your way through the maze to the mummy's tomb?

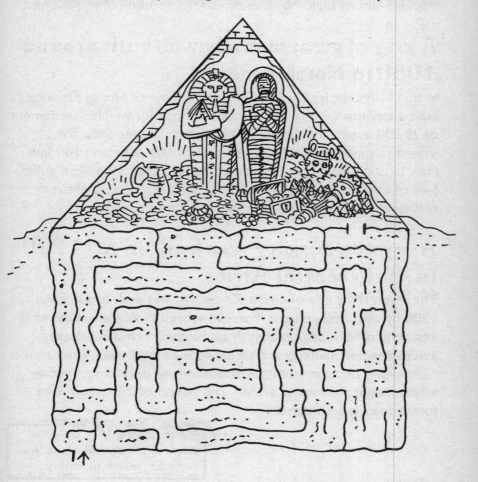

Solution, see page 142

An Arab ruler founded a translation service in AD 830.

Caliph Abdullah al-Ma'mun founded the House of Wisdom in Baghdad to translate works by Greek scientists and philosophers into Arabic. Later, the Arabic translations were translated still once more, this time into Latin. This led to the revival of learning in Europe. The caliph's interest in the arts and sciences also inspired him to build observatories for the study of astronomy.

A city of great mounds was built around 1050 in North America.

In the 11th century, the Mississippian people of North America built a city made up of enormous earth platforms. This settlement of 20,000 inhabitants included more than 100 mounds. The largest mound (Monks Mound) was 160 feet wide and 100 feet high. In order to create the mounds, more than 50 million cubic feet of earth had to be moved. This city, the largest prehistoric settlement north of Mexico, was near Cahokia, Illinois.

A mysterious city was built in AD 1200 in south central Africa.

The mysterious city of Great Zimbabwe was built around AD 1200 by the Shona people. For 300 years, it was the center of a vast empire in south central Africa. Nothing remains except massive stone buildings and an abandoned gold mine. The name "Zimbabwe" comes from the Shona phrase *dzimba dza mabwe*, which means "houses of stone." The nation of Zimbabwe was formerly called Rhodesia.

FAST FACT Genghis Khan controlled more land than any other person in history.

By the year 1215, most of Asia was under the rule of nomads from Mongolia.

The Mongols were superb archers and horsemen, and they rode out of central Asia to conquer much of the known world. The empire of Genghis Khan and, later, his sons, extended from Hungary to Korea.

The Standout Soldier

Find the one Mongol soldier who is different from the others.

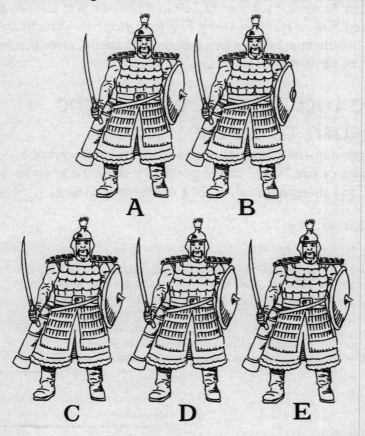

A   B

C   D   E

Solution, see page 142

Hospital administrators founded the German state of Prussia.

The Order of Teutonic Knights was originally organized in 1226, to maintain hospitals and to care for pilgrims in the Holy Land. It became a military organization that conquered the lands around the Baltic Sea, including the territory that later became Prussia.

The first female Muslim ruler governed in 1236.

Princess Raziyya, daughter of Sultan Iltutmish, was chosen to succeed him as ruler in Delhi. For four years she fought to keep her throne, leading her troops into battle, until she was killed in 1240.

The lack of salt caused the English to riot in 1316.

In England in 1316, riots occurred after the country had a shortage of salt. To add to the people's misery, the grain harvest failed, and sheep began dying of a mysterious disease.

FAST FACT Words in English that trace back to Quechua, the official language of the Incan Empire, include "condor," "quinine," and "puma." Quechua is still spoken by more than 10 million people in South America.

One hundred and eighty soldiers conquered an empire of 10 million people.

Francisco Pizarro

The Incan Empire of 10 million people in South America stretched for 3,000 miles from Ecuador to Chile and Argentina. In 1532, the Spanish adventurer Francisco Pizarro landed in South America with a small band of soldiers numbering 180. The gold-hungry Pizarro kidnapped the Incan emperor Atahualpa. After a large room was filled with gold as the emperor's ransom, Pizarro went back on his word and murdered Atahualpa. The great Incan Empire soon came to an end.

Tangled Explorers

Can you unscramble these words that are related the Incan Empire?

1. hualpaata
2. echli
3. lodg
4. acin
5. arrpizo

Solution, see page 142

America is named after an Italian navigator and traveler.

The name America was taken from Italian traveler Amerigo Vespucci, who authored a popular book about his travels. Christopher Columbus was ignored. Also, though Vespucci did not discover the area covered by the United States, it is believed that he made it to parts of South America.

Christopher Columbus

Indians got their name by mistake.

When Christopher Columbus reached the Americas in 1492, he thought he had reached India. So, he called the people he met Indians. Today, we use the term Native Americans or American Indians.

Three presidents have their faces on both coins and bills.

Abraham Lincoln appears on both the penny and the $5 bill. Thomas Jefferson is on the nickel and the $2 bill. George Washington appears on both the quarter and the $1 bill.

Pennsylvania had the first circulating library in the United States.

Benjamin Franklin organized the country's first circulating library in 1731, in Philadelphia, Pennsylvania. The first children's book department in a public library was set up in Minneapolis, Minnesota, in 1892. The very first American library was established in 1698, in Charlotte, South Carolina.

FAST FACT Benjamin Franklin is credited with the invention of the rocking chair.

Dime Rhymes

Is a poem about a coin a "dime rhyme?" Just add the missing word for a rhyme.

1. Sweet cent   honey _____

2. Money expert   _____ scholar

3. Steal a quarter   purloin _____

4. Show off bankroll   flash _____

COLONIAL AMERICANS ATE WELL, BUT SIMPLY.

The foods of colonial America included corn fritters, hoecake, hominy, johnnycake, maple sugar mush, shoofly pie, and succotash. Hoecakes were made from cornmeal and were baked on the flat blade of a hoe. Johnnycakes are flat bread made from cornmeal. Shoofly pie is a very sweet pie made with crumbs, butter, and brown sugar. It would attract flies that would then have to be shooed, or chased away, which is how it got its name.

SALEM, MASSACHUSETTS, AND NEWPORT, RHODE ISLAND, WERE AMONG THE LARGEST AMERICAN CITIES IN 1790.

In order of population, the largest U.S. cities were Philadelphia (42,444), New York City (33,131), Boston, Massachusetts (18,038), Charlestown, Massachusetts (16,359), Salem, Massachusetts (7,921), and Newport, Rhode Island (6,716).

THE PIONEERS USED MANY UNUSUAL TOOLS.

Among the strange tools that pioneers needed were a corn knife, a flail, a grain cradle, a froe (a cleaving tool), a hog scraper, hoof files, (a type of pick axe), sack needles, and spoke shavers. A well-furnished pioneer home would have a candle snuffer, lard press, quilting frame, sausage gun, skin stretchers, splint broom, and wooden trenchers (platters).

FAST FACT Until the Civil War, there were no admirals in the U.S. Navy. The highest rank was commodore. In 1862, the rank of rear admiral was created. It was first bestowed on Captain David G. Farragut.

SOME OF THE WEAPONS USED IN THE CIVIL WAR (1861–1865) WERE EXPERIMENTAL.

Both the Union and the Confederacy experimented with such weapons as the Minié rifle (named for Claude Minié, a French officer), the Gatling gun, the garrison cannon, the naval swivel cannon, and the revolving rifle. The Civil War also saw the first-time use of aerial photographs, an ambulance corps, a cigarette tax, flame throwers, hospital ships, income tax, machine gun, military draft, nursing corps, and smoke screen.

Terms introduced in the Civil War include AWOL, doughboy, draftee, the Medal of Honor, pup tent, skedaddle, unconditional surrender, and war correspondent.

Go West!

Can you find your way across the country to California?

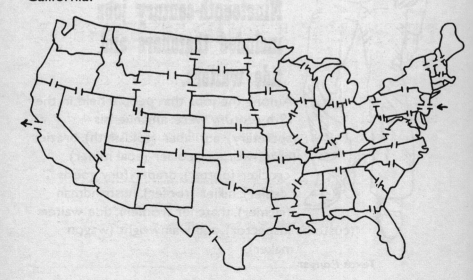

Solution, see page 142

Originally, there were only 10 Texas Rangers.

The Texas Rangers were organized in the 1830s by the Texas pioneer Stephen F. Austin. There were just 10 men in the first mounted force.

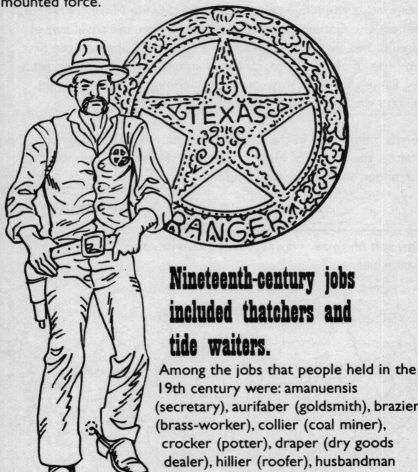

Nineteenth-century jobs included thatchers and tide waiters.

Among the jobs that people held in the 19th century were: amanuensis (secretary), aurifaber (goldsmith), brazier (brass-worker), collier (coal miner), crocker (potter), draper (dry goods dealer), hillier (roofer), husbandman (farmer), thatcher (roofer), tide waiter (customs inspector), and wainwright (wagon maker).

Texas Ranger

In 1906, people drove Cadillacs, Buicks, and Fords. They also drove Maxwells and Zents.

Among the cars sold in 1906 were these makes: Autocar, Cannon, Compound, Corbin, Crawford, Dolson, Duquesne, Duryea, Elmore, Gale, Jackson, Michigan, Northern, Oxford, Pierce, Reo, and the Wolverine. Twenty-five years later, in the 1930s, most of the early car makes had disappeared. Instead, people were driving cars called Auburns, Cords, Duesenbergs, Grahams, Hudsons, Hupmobiles, LaFayettes, LaSalles, Oaklands, Rocknes, Stutzes, and Terraplanes.

FAST FACT For a short while, both the Franklin and the Roosevelt were makes of car.

Old-fashioned Jobs

Some people in the 19th century had job titles that sound strange today. Can you match the job with the job title?

1. amanuensis	brass-worker
2. aurifaber	coal miner
3. brazier	customs inspector
4. collier	dry goods dealer
5. crocker	farmer
6. draper	goldsmith
7. husbandman	potter
8. thatcher	roofer
9. tide waiter	secretary
10. wainwright	wagon maker

Solution, see page 143

THERE WERE FIVE FIVE-STAR GENERALS IN WORLD WAR II (1939–1945).

The five-star generals in World War II included Omar N. Bradley, Dwight D. Eisenhower, Douglas MacArthur, George C. Marshall, and Henry "Hap" Arnold.

General Dwight D. Eisenhower

SHOES WERE RATIONED DURIN' WORLD WAR II.

Rationed items included butter, canned foods, cheese, coffee, fats, gasoline, meats, oils, and sugar. Rationing means making sure there's enough of scarce items to go around. It's sometimes done in war time, or after a natural disaster such as a hurricane or tornado.

A 1704 NEWSPAPER CARRIED THE FIRST AMERICAN CLASSIFIED ADS.

The first ads appeared in the *Boston News-Letter* on May 18, 1704. They were tiny little notices, more like our classified ads. One ad offered a mill for rent or sale in Oyster Bay, Long Island, "in the Province of New York." Another ad offered a reward for the capture of a thief. The third ad was a notice that two anvils were missing from a smithy. In the 1730s, Benjamin Franklin (1706–1790) made ads more readable by printing them with large headlines, the way we do today.

THE FIRST AMERICAN TOLL ROAD WAS IN VIRGINIA.

The Little River Turnpike of 1785 was the first toll road in America. It led from Alexandria to Bluemont and Snicker's (Snigger's) Gap in the Blue Ridge Mountains.

Names in General

The five five-star generals of World War II sometimes would sign their names in big letters. Not all of their names could fit on the documents they signed. Part of their first name is on the top line and part of their second name is on the bottom. Using the word list, can you figure out who is who?

> Douglas MacArthur   Dwight D. Eisenhower
> George C. Marshall   Henry "Hap" Arnold
> Omar Bradley

1. mar
   rad

2. wig
   how

3. las
   cAr

4. eor
   rsh

5. Hen
   old

Blaise Pascal

The bus was invented in 1662, by a French philosopher.

Blaise Pascal, philosopher and mathematician, invented the bus in 1662. However, it took almost 200 years for the world to catch up with his invention. It was only in 1847 that the first "omnibus" was introduced, and even then it was horse-drawn.

Women have invented many important everyday objects.

Tabitha Babbitt invented the circular saw in 1812. Mary Anderson invented the windshield wiper in 1904. Patsy Sherman invented Scotchgard (1955). Bette Nesmith Graham invented Liquid Paper; originally called Mistake Out (1956), and Randi Altschul invented the disposable cell phone (1999).

Thomas Edison (1847–1931) invented the cement mixer.

He also invented an early voting machine, the phonograph, the electric lightbulb, the motion-picture projector, the storage battery, and the electric utility company.

The first man to sail alone around the world couldn't swim a stroke.

Captain Joshua Slocum (1844–1909) sailed around the world by himself in 1895, the first to do so. The non-swimmer's 46,000-mile voyage took three years in a vessel that was less than 37 feet long. On November 14, 1909, Slocum set out on another solo trip. He left from Martha's Vineyard and was headed to South America. He never made it there and was never heard from again.

FAST FACT A successful invention of Blaise Pascal's was the first mechanical adding machine. He invented it when he was 21, for his father, who was a tax official.

Find Edison's Inventions

Edison invented many things. See how many you can find in the grid below. Look down and across.

BATTERY
LIGHTBULB
PHONOGRAPH
PROJECTOR

P	H	O	N	O	G	R	A	P	H
R	L	I	G	H	T	B	U	L	B
O	W	F	B	J	K	L	B	N	M
J	U	V	A	F	Q	R	E	W	T
E	A	Q	T	P	O	K	H	T	J
C	M	H	T	D	F	G	H	P	L
T	Y	H	E	Q	D	A	S	W	E
O	Z	X	R	C	V	B	G	H	R
R	J	H	Y	T	L	K	J	H	F

Solution, see page 143

The first women to work for the U.S. government were paid 50¢ a day.

Sara Waldrake and Rachael Summers were hired in 1795, by the U.S. Mint in Philadelphia, Pennsylvania, to weigh gold coins, at 50¢ a day.

Part of Antarctica is named for a U.S. Navy lieutenant.

In 1838, Lieutenant Charles Wilkes, USN, commanded the first scientific expedition in U.S. history. Lt. Wilkes's mission was to survey the South Seas. The total cost of the expedition was $150,000. The expedition reached a part of Antarctica on January 16, 1840, which was later named Wilkes Land. The expedition collected penguins, proved that Antarctica was a continent, charted almost 300 Pacific islands, and sailed around the world.

The first fingerprint technician was appointed in 1903.

John M. Shea of the St. Louis Police Department was appointed superintendent of the Bertillion system (a fingerprinting method) on September 14, 1903. He remained at the post until 1926.

A U.S. Army colonel was the defendant in the first U.S. military court martial.

The first American military court martial was held on January 20, 1778, in Cambridge, Massachusetts. Colonel David Henley, commander of U.S. troops in Cambridge, was accused of conduct unbecoming an officer. He was found not guilty.

Robert E. Lee almost led the Union forces.

Before the Civil War, Robert E. Lee was one of the U.S. Army's most highly regarded officers. In fact, Abraham Lincoln offered him field command of the Union army in April 1861. A few days later, however, Lee accepted command of the forces of his home state, Virginia, which had seceded from the Union.

FAST FACT After the Civil War, Robert E. Lee became the president of Washington College. Today it is known as Washington and Lee University.

Penguin Pairs

Can you find the two penguins in this group that are exactly alike?

A   B   C

D   E

Solution, see page 143

IAN FLEMING, CREATOR OF "007" (JAMES BOND), WAS HIMSELF A SECRET AGENT.

Ian Fleming

Spy novelist Ian Fleming knew what he was writing about. During World War II, he was a British naval intelligence officer in charge of a special unit with the dangerous mission of obtaining secret German codebooks and equipment. His real-life experiences in espionage gave him material for his books.

A NIGHTMARE INSPIRED THE HORROR NOVEL JEKYLL AND HYDE.

Author Robert Louis Stevenson wrote the famous horror novel *The Strange Case of Dr. Jekyll and Mr. Hyde* in three days. He had a nightmare that gave him the plot. Actually, it was based on a real-life crime story. A respected member of the community was secretly the leader of a gang of thieves. He was finally caught and hanged. Stevenson remembered the story and dreamed about it.

FAST FACT Robert Louis Stevenson did much of his writing in bed.

BEFORE HE BECAME PRESIDENT IN 1829, ANDREW JACKSON FOUGHT IN A DUEL AND WAS SHOT.

The duel was in 1806. Andrew Jackson was hit in the chest. He staggered, gritted his teeth, and shot his opponent, Charles Dickinson, and killed him. Later, Jackson said that he planned to kill this man with a single bullet, even "if he had shot me through the brain." Because the bullet was too close to Jackson's heart, it was never removed, and he carried it for the rest of his life.

Jumbled Presidents

Un-jumble these presidential clues to get the names of four presidents. For example: Which President wasn't a vote loser? Answer: Theodore or Franklin Roosevelt. "Vote loser" is a scrambled version of "Roosevelt."

President List: Andrew Jackson, Franklin Pierce, James Madison, Jimmy Carter

1. Which dueling president may have warned his opponents that he was a good shot?

2. Which president, when he was a naval officer, probably saw tracer bullets?

3. Which president may have had a favorite recipe that the White House chef prepared?

4. Which president watched out for our country's possessions and domains?

Solution, see page 143

These two famous Americans were born on the same day, 12 years apart.

Babe Ruth, perhaps baseball's greatest all-around player, was born on February 6, 1895. Baltimore Orioles owner Jack Dunn paid Ruth $600 for his first season in 1914, shortly after his 19th birthday. Ruth got his nickname when some old-timer sneered at the young rookie's baby face, saying "Here's another of Dunn's babes."

Ronald Reagan, 40th president of the United States, was born in Tampico, Illinois, on February 6, 1911. Reagan was strongly influenced by his mother, who taught him to read at an early age. In 1936, he became a sportscaster for station WHO in Des Moines, Iowa, and in the movies played a famous football hero, George "The Gipper" Gipp.

One of the most successful families of American actors is the Barrymores.

The Barrymore family is made up of actors and actresses who have had major success in the theater and in the movies. Drew Barrymore is the most current member of the successful family. Her grandfather was the great actor John Barrymore Sr., who appeared in more than 30 films. Oscar-winner Lionel Barrymore was her great-uncle and Oscar-winner Ethel Barrymore was her great-aunt. Her great-grandfather, Maurice Barrymore, was also a distinguished actor. Her great-great grandmother, Louisa Drew, was a celebrated actress of the 1820s.

FAST FACT The Barrymore family of actors inspired the 1927 play *The Royal Family* by Edna Ferber and George S. Kaufman.

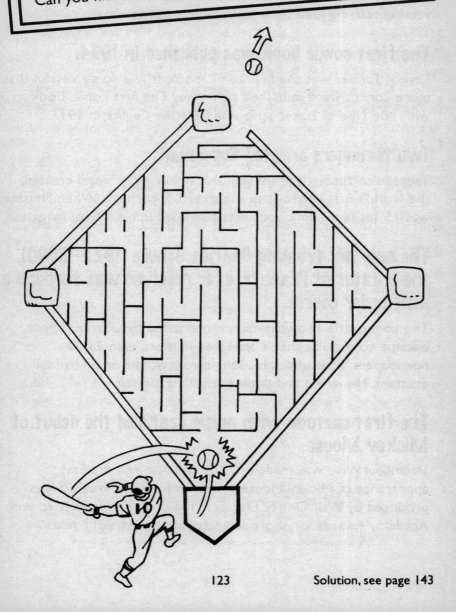

Play Ball!

Can you hit a home run out of this baseball maze?

Solution, see page 143

The Wizard of Oz was first a stage musical.

The Wizard of Oz was produced in 1902, as a stage musical. The first movie version was a silent production in 1925. The 1939 version starring Judy Garland became a movie classic.

The first comic book was published in 1934.

Famous Funnies was the first comic book. It was so successful that more comics were published right away. The first comic book with one type of comic strip was *Detective Comics*, in 1937.

Two teenagers created Superman.

Teenage cartoonist Joe Shuster and writer Jerry Siegel created the world's first comic-strip superhero, Superman. When Shuster was 15, his first comic strip was published in his school magazine.

The only art training Charles Schulz (1922–2000), the creator of Peanuts, ever received was through a mail-order course.

The comic strip *Peanuts*, which was created by Charles Schulz, became so popular that it appeared in more than 2,000 newspapers. Throughout his long career, Schulz never had an assistant. He wrote and drew everything himself.

The first cartoon with music featured the debut of Mickey Mouse.

Steamboat Willie was made in 1928, and featured the first appearance of Mickey Mouse. It also had a music track. It was produced by Walt Disney. Disney is the only moviemaker to win Academy Awards for short subjects for eight straight years.

Ever dream about creating your own superhero? Now is your chance. Draw a superhero on the cover below.

FAST FACT The first American movie cartoon was *Humorous Phases of Funny Faces*. It was released in 1906.

Solution, see page 143

Seven college sports teams are called the Blue Devils.

The Blue Devils name is shared by Central Connecticut State, Dillard University, Duke University, Lawrence Institute of Technology, Philadelphia College of Pharmacy and Science, the State University College of New York (Fredonia), and the University of Wisconsin, Stout.

Eight college teams are known as the Bear Cats; 19 are called the Bears; 32 are called the Bulldogs; 18 are called the Cougars. There are 23 college teams called the Crusaders; 30 are called the Eagles (nine are called the Golden Eagles); 23 are called the Lions; 12 are called the Owls; 23 are the Panthers; 40 teams are called the Tigers; and 22 are called the Wildcats.

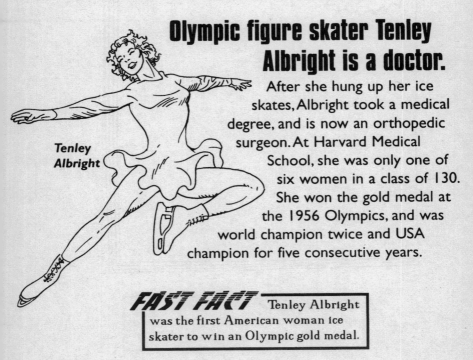

Olympic figure skater Tenley Albright is a doctor.

After she hung up her ice skates, Albright took a medical degree, and is now an orthopedic surgeon. At Harvard Medical School, she was only one of six women in a class of 130. She won the gold medal at the 1956 Olympics, and was world champion twice and USA champion for five consecutive years.

Tenley Albright

FAST FACT Tenley Albright was the first American woman ice skater to win an Olympic gold medal.

Only one baseball manager won World Series in both leagues.

Sparky Anderson managed World Series winners Cincinnati in 1975 to 1976 and Detroit in 1984. He is also the only manager to win 100 games in both leagues.

Boxer Henry Armstrong was the only boxer to hold world titles at three weight divisions at the same time.

Henry Armstrong (1912–1988) was the simultaneous champion in featherweight, welterweight, and lightweight divisions. Armstrong retired from boxing in 1945, and became a Baptist minister.

Team Play

Part of each of these college teams has vanished. Can you find the missing section in the word part list?

Word part list: ANT, BUL, DCA, OUG, USA

1. W I L __ __ __ T S
2. C __ __ __ A R S
3. C R __ __ __ D E R S
4. P __ __ __ H E R S
5. __ __ __ L D O G S

Rick Barry was the only player to win scoring titles in both the National Basketball Association (NBA) and the American Basketball Association (ABA).

The basketball great also holds the second all-time highest free-throw percentage (.900). In his 12-year career span (1967–1979), he was an all-star five times.

Boris Becker was the youngest male Wimbledon champ.

The German tennis player won at Wimbledon at age 17, becoming the youngest male player to win a singles title at Wimbledon.

Basketball coach Clair Bee wrote 23 books for children.

Clair Bee's Chip Hilton basketball novels for children number 23. He also wrote 21 nonfiction basketball books. He originated the 1-3-1 defense, and is in the Basketball Hall of Fame in Springfield, Massachusetts.

Catcher Yogi Berra played on 10 World Series-winning teams.

He is the all-time series leader in games, at-bats, singles, and doubles. He was also manager of the pennant-winning New York Yankees (1964) and New York Mets (1973).

FAST FACT In his career, George Blanda scored 2,002 points—the highest total in professional football history.

George Blanda retired at 48, the oldest man ever to play pro football.

Blanda played in 340 games over 26 seasons as a member of four different teams in two leagues. Blanda was the only player to lead both the National Football League (NFL) and the American Football League (AFL) in pass completions.

George Blanda

Active Reading

Clair Bee wrote 23 books on basketball. What sport do you think each book is about?

1. *The Case of the Unstrung Crossbow* _____

2. *The Mystery of the Shuffling Shuttlecock* _____

3. *The Riddle of the Stolen Bases* _____

4. *The Jumpshot Jinx* _____

5. *The Springboard Secret* _____

6. *The Forward Pass File* _____

7. *The Horror of the Hole-in-One* _____

8. *The Face-Off Fantasy* _____

Sports: diving, golf, ice hockey, badminton, football, basketball, baseball, archery

Solution, see page 144

Pro basketball forward Bill Bradley was a Rhodes Scholar and, later, a U.S. senator.

Bradley played on two NBA championship teams. At Princeton, he was an All-American basketball player. He was named college player of the year in 1965. He joined the Knicks as a forward in 1967. He later became a U.S. senator from New Jersey.

Star running back Byron "Whizzer" White became a Supreme Court justice.

White was a star running back on the University of Colorado football team. He then joined the Pittsburgh Steelers, leading the National Football League (NFL) in rushing in his first year. He played football for the Detroit Lions while in law school. He became a lawyer, and was named justice to the U.S. Supreme Court in 1962, serving until 1993.

A star Michigan football center became president.

After graduating from the University of Michigan, college all-star Jerry Ford was offered contracts by the Detroit Lions and the Green Bay Packers. He turned them down and became a lawyer and a politician. As Richard M. Nixon's vice president, he succeeded to the presidency when Nixon resigned.

A former professional quarterback ran for vice president.

A former quarterback with the San Diego Chargers and Buffalo Bills, Jack Kemp later became a congressman and secretary of housing and urban development under President George H. W. Bush. He ran for vice president on the unsuccessful ticket of presidential nominee Robert Dole in 1996.

Political Touchdown

Help this football player achieve his goal of political stardom. Show him the way to higher office and help him avoid the traps along the way that will lead him to a dead end.

FAST FACT

Bill Bradley became a U.S. senator in 1978. At the time, he was 35 years old and was the youngest senator in the Senate.

Solution, see page 144

Yale's football coach created the quarterback position.

Walter Camp (1859–1925), a turn-of-the-century football authority, and head football coach at Yale, made football the game it is today. In addition to creating the quarterback position, he helped define the rules of football, invented the system of downs, and set the number of players at 11. In 1889, he also invented the college All-American team.

A 14-year-old Romanian gymnast was the first to score a perfect 10 in the Olympics.

When Nadia Comaneci was six years old, she became a student of famed Romanian gymnastics coach Bela Karolyi. Eight years later, at the 1976 Summer Olympics, Nadia Comaneci became the first gymnast to receive a perfect score from the judges, earning a 10.00 in the uneven bars event.

Baseball's Grapefruit League is in Florida.

Major league teams that conduct spring training and play exhibition games in Florida are called the Grapefruit League. The first team to train in Florida was the 1888 Washington Nationals.

FAST FACT Walter Camp's other football innovations include the scrimmage line and offensive signal calling.

A 19-year-old Californian was the first woman to win tennis's grand slam.

Maureen "Little Mo" Connolly, was the first woman to win the grand slam of tennis—the Australian championships, the French championships, Wimbledon, and the United States championships—in one calendar year, 1953.

She was the second player in history to earn the grand slam. (American player Don Budge was the first in 1938.)

Maureen "Little Mo" Connolly

Football Plays

How many words can you make out of FOOTBALL? We found 19.

FOOTBALL

_____ _____ _____

_____ _____ _____

_____ _____ _____

_____ _____ _____

_____ _____ .

_____ _____

Solution, see page 144

SOLUTIONS

Page 3
1. captors = raptors
2. egos = eggs   3. planes = plants
4. hard = herd   5. corns = horns

Page 5

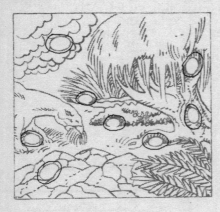

Page 7
1. bee
2. spider
3. fly
4. ant
5. cockroach

Page 9
1. crabapple
2. crabby
3. crabgrass
4. crabwise

Page 11
1. angler strangler
2. viper swiper
3. snake steak
4. tooth booth
5. battler rattler

Page 13
B is the real catfish.

Page 15
1. tern
2. hen
3. owl
4. crow
5. gull
6. teal
7. eagle
8. egret
9. raven
10. robin

Page 17
1. ear = bear
2. mine = ermine
3. and = eland
4. ink = mink
5. came = camel
6. easel = weasel

SOLUTIONS

Page 19
1. collie
2. boxer
3. chihuahua
4. greyhound

Page 21
1. burmese, siamese, and persian
2. manx
3. domestic tabby, tortoiseshell, and turkish angora

Page 23

Page 25

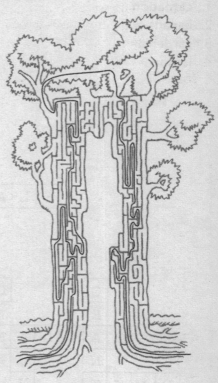

Page 27
A. fog
B. rare
C. stern

forest ranger

Page 29
1. iris 2. sage 3. spruce
4. poppy 5. hop

SOLUTIONS

Page 31
1. carnation
2. banana
3. gardenia
4. lemon

Page 33

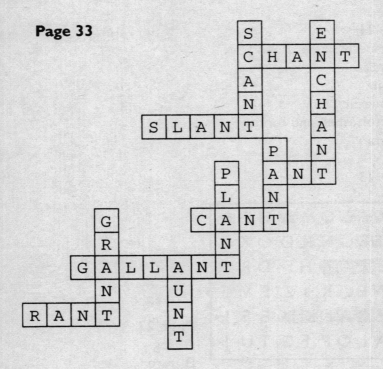

Page 35
"Scramble" = boil

Page 37
1. chocolate
2. avocado
3. bread
4. popcorn
5. bean

SOLUTIONS

Page 39
1. star 2. galaxy 3. planet
4. satellite

Page 41
1. spaceship 2. Odin
3. purple grape

Page 43

Page 45
1. sunbelt 2. sunspot
3. sunbonnet 4. sunrise

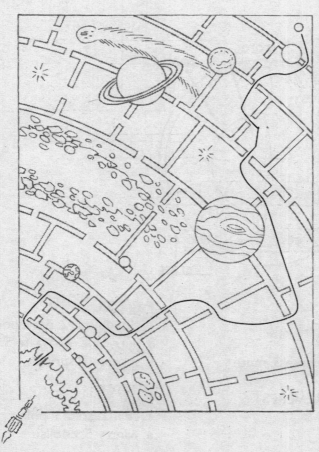

SOLUTIONS

Page 47

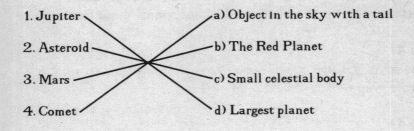

1. Jupiter
2. Asteroid
3. Mars
4. Comet

a) Object in the sky with a tail
b) The Red Planet
c) Small celestial body
d) Largest planet

Page 49

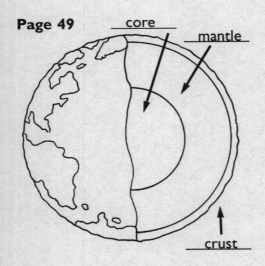

core

mantle

crust

Page 53

1. cloudburst 2. downpour
3. hurricane 4. irrigate 5. rainfall
6. shower 7. sprinkle

Page 51

1. ton 2. verse 3. mute

MOUNT EVEREST

Page 55

1. chill 2. cold 3. polar
4. wintry 5. coolish

SOLUTIONS

Page 57
1. The snow bank 2. In hot pursuit
3. A spinning rod

Page 59
lariat, lariats, last, liar, rat, rats,
sail, star, suit, tail, tails, tar, tars,
trail, trails

Page 61

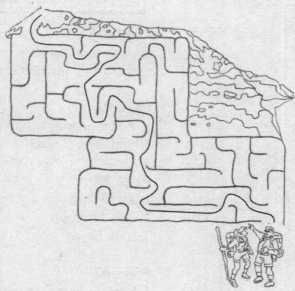

Page 63
1. shell – sell 2. drain – rain
3. sink – ink 4. drag – rag

Page 65
1. quick + silver = quicksilver
(mercury)   2. pla**TIN**um
3. **PAL**ladium 4. **RUTH**enium

Page 67
1. cruise's fuses 2. rocket
socket 3. wire buyer
4. dark spark

Page 69
a) Bakelite b) celluloid
c) rayon d) acetate

Page 71
1. oil painting 2. salad oil
3. oilers 4. burn the midnight oil
5. snake oil

SOLUTIONS

Page 73
1. bacteria 2. protozoa
3. mushroom 4. rose 5. cow

Page 75
1. a 2. c 3. b

Page 77

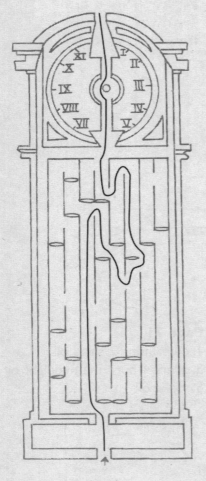

Page 79

H	I	G	H	W	A	Y	X
T	D	Z	M	R	V	Q	B
M	J	L	A	N	E	T	A
A	I	E	O	D	N	Z	U
E	B	X	T	U	U	P	L
A	S	T	R	E	E	T	C

Page 81
a) channel b) cable
c) sitcom d) Sesame Street

Page 83
1. mouse 2. program 3. keyboard
4. hard drive 5. pixel

Page 85
1. air bag
2. man in moon
3. stale bread

Page 87
1. heart – hear 2. bone – one
3. face – ace 4. hand – and
5. heel – eel 6. skin – kin
7. brain – rain 8. gland – land
9. spine – spin 10. liver – live
11. thigh – high
12. pelvis – Elvis

SOLUTIONS

Page 89
1. forehead 2. gullet
3. eardrum 4. tonsil

Page 91
1. hair 2. scalp 3. keratin
4. beard

Page 93
C and E are exactly alike.

Page 95

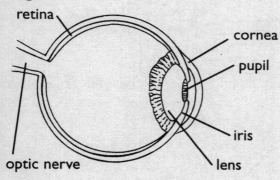

retina
cornea
pupil
iris
lens
optic nerve

Page 97

Page 99
1. appaloosa 2. arabian
3. clydesdale 4. morgan
5. percheron 6. shetland

Page 101
1. words 2. Egyptians
3. alphabet 4. dictionary
5. Phoenicians 6. turn
7. writing
mystery word: reading

SOLUTIONS

Page 103

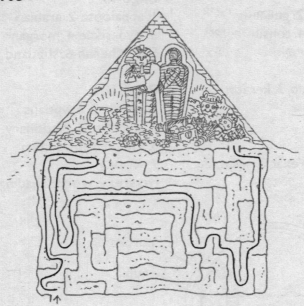

Page 105
Soldier B is different.

Page 107
1. Atahualpa
2. Chile
3. gold
4. Inca
5. Pizarro

Page 109
1. honey money 2. dollar
scholar 3. purloin coin
4. flash cash

Page 111

SOLUTIONS

Page 113
1. secretary 2. goldsmith
3. brass-worker 4. coal miner
5. potter 6. dry goods dealer
7. farmer 8. roofer
9. customs inspector
10. wagon maker

Page 115
1. Omar Bradley 2. Dwight D.
Eisenhower 3. Douglas
MacArthur 4. George C.
Marshall 5. Henry "Hap" Arnold

Page 117

Page 119
Penguins A and D

Page 121
1. Andrew (Jackson) 2. (Jimmy)
Carter 3. (Franklin) Pierce
4. (James) Madison

Page 123

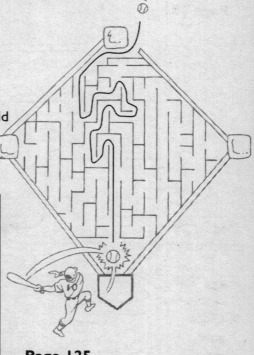

Page 125
Answers will vary

Page 127
1 wildcats 2. cougars
3. crusaders 4. panthers
5. bulldogs

SOLUTIONS

Page 129
1. archery 2. badminton
3. baseball 4. basketball
5. diving 6. football 7. golf
8. ice hockey

Page 133
ball, blot, bloat, boat, boll, boot,
fall, fat, flab, flat, float, foot, lab,
lob, loot, tab, tall, toll, too

Page 131